IRMA K
TEN-POI
• • • • •
FOR AN UNT

Also by Irma Kurtz

IRMA KURTZ'S
TEN-POINT PLAN

· · · · · · · · · ·

FOR AN UNTROUBLED LIFE

Irma Kurtz

FOURTH ESTATE • *London*

To Midge, for her courage and friendship

First published in Great Britain in 1995 by
Fourth Estate Limited
6 Salem Road
London W2 4BU

A catalogue record for this book is available from the British Library.

ISBN 1 85702 333 1

Typeset from Author's Disc by SX Composing Ltd, Rayleigh, Essex
Printed in Great Britain by Cox & Wyman Ltd, Reading, Berks.

CONTENTS

INTRODUCTION

I am what's known as an 'agony aunt'. I prefer to be called 'agony aunt' rather than by a more impressive title. Agony aunt describes very well my role on *Cosmopolitan* magazine: agony aunt is what I am — older than most of the people who consult me, I am concerned, sometimes moved, often annoyed, always ready to put in my two cents' worth as a good auntie should. Without any formal training, without dogma, participating in no school of thought, I am not expert in very much more than I have seen first-hand or done, and sometimes in no more than I have dreamed. Endless curiosity and an irrepressible compulsion to communicate what I am thinking are probably the two highest qualifications for this job.

Nosy and bossy, in other words, are what you have to be in my line of work. And, on a good day, possessed of an imagination that finds itself instantly at home in the skin of another human being, even on the basis of no more than a few pages, generally hand-written, to *Cosmopolitan*'s resident agony aunt. But I am not an infallible know-it-all claiming purchase on every emotional hiccough of mere mortals. What I most definitely am not is a psychologist, psychiatrist or therapist. Can you imagine sitting silently hour after hour listening to accusations and complaints? It would bore me rigid, and frustrate me beyond belief not to be able to give a spontaneous opinion on what I was hearing. My *opinion* is what I offer the people who write to me, not a moral stricture; nor, properly speaking, am I hawking remedies — certainly I do not expect anyone to do what I say, merely to *hear* what I say and then, having heard, do as she decides she must.

The trouble with trouble is that as soon as a body is in the middle of it, and deranged by pain or anger, she loses sight of the countless possibilities between 'either' and 'or', 'stay' and 'go', 'yes' and 'no'. She is no longer able to distinguish any of the colours or shades between black and white. All any agony aunt or any friend can do is point out from a more detached viewpoint choices the troubled woman cannot see from the rollercoaster she is on. Or (and I'm afraid this is still more likely) you can remind her of the choices she does not *wish* to see and will not see. Why won't she see them? Because they are the least pretty alternatives, the most difficult, the most solitary, and probably the only ones of any use in the long run. If all the answers to all our problems were pleasant, who would need an agony aunt or anyone else to help them choose?

Hope is a virtue, to be sure, but if living a relatively untroubled life has an antithesis, it is the kind of wishful thinking that outstays hope and makes an ass of reason. One lesson I have learned from this job is that mankind in general, and more specifically womankind, has a practically unlimited capacity for self-delusion.

'He'll change after we're married', for instance.

Or, 'Of course he still loves me, he has sex with me, doesn't he?'

Or, 'He broke my heart, it's over. All I want is for us to stay friends . . .'

To all of which this agony aunt can but reply, 'Fat chance!'

You'd be surprised how many of the problems that come my way on *Cosmo*'s Agony column strike a chord, because I too have been there in my time and, more than once — believe me — made a mess of things. I have never married (never saw the point of it); I have had a child (well-planned but out of wedlock); I have been with men I did not really love and loved men whom I did not very much like. In my time I've gone to bed with men I hardly knew, and I've sent letters I wished I hadn't; once I was involved with another woman's husband — not a mistake I repeated. Many years ago I had to have an abortion. And until the world is a place of perfect chance and charity, I must endorse the need for free and legal terminations.

Has my own private life been a perpetual building site? Who am I to say? Agony aunts are not members of the clergy: moral judgements are not my department. Reason, not a moral code, is my base: what *is*, never what should be. Mind you, telling people what is, is not always politically correct, but telling them what they should do is hardly ever ethical.

'You should' between individuals too often translates as 'I want'. And 'why should I?', if we were honest, would rarely have a reply more genuine or less stupid than, 'because I say so'. That's why I try consciously to avoid the word 'should' in my replies to letters and in my everyday conversation, except in its conditional sense.

It is not necessary for us agony aunts to have led blameless lives, and frankly, it would not be very smart of a troubled woman to seek earthy advice from an angel. You do not need to be good in order to become wise. On the contrary, no spirited woman has ever stayed out of trouble, or ever will. Trouble is part of the price we pay for freedom, but getting out of trouble, and staying out of the same damn trouble again and again and again is the reward of experience. Experience taken to heart in due course becomes wisdom; and wisdom is a gift designed for sharing.

I am very, very careful to share my honest opinion only with those I love or when I'm paid for it: I write for my living, after all. In my role as agony aunt I have a vast readership on several continents. It constantly astonishes me that so many people read my words and pay attention to them, but as long as they do, I intend to say exactly what I mean, and to say it as well as I can. To say anything I do not mean or say it less well than I am able would be a waste of my time and yours.

Want to solve your own problems? If a one-hundred-per-cent born romantic like me has learned how to learn from experience, then so can you, or anyone. You need first to accumulate your own body of experience, and then add to it all you have ever observed or read or heard about the experiences of others.

Gossip has a bad name, and malicious gossip is truly foul, because malice is heartless and always judgemental. Malicious gossip reinforces prejudice without any increase whatsoever in understanding. However, the perpetual sifting and exchanging of views on each other's lives — call it 'benevolent gossip' — is an ancient and honourable way by which women in particular have learned and taught each other about life since old wives were young and telling their very first tales. Creative gossip, constantly observing, analysing and comparing, uncovers some basic truths about human behaviour and gives general rules to apply in our private lives, rules that are no less valid because exceptions exist.

Is it not perfectly true, for instance, to say that married men continue not to leave their wives a lot more often than they leave 'em? And whatever that straying husband whispers in your ear, his wife, or another wife in the same spot, has written to me, and I'll give you ten to one he still makes love to her (if only on holidays and special occasions). If you stay with a violent man, don't be surprised when he hits you. Excessive jealousy can actually create the infidelity it dreads (why not be hanged for a sheep?). No eighteen-year-old is ever as mature as she thinks she is (to think herself mature at eighteen is in itself immature).

Most of what agony aunts have to say is common sense. Common sense is a defensive skill, acquired rather than inspired, and generally peace-loving. It is based on reason and observation. What is common sense if not a garden variety of logic? And one root of science. Don't undersell common sense. It is available to all, yet practised by very few, and it has counted just as much as imagination and ingenuity for our survival on this planet.

Nevertheless, it would be pointless to reject classic dogma only to become dogmatic about common sense. Love, for example, rarely makes much sense, common or uncommon. (Never sneeze at luck as a very important element of love.) And come the crunch, *any* commitment whatsoever — to a mate, to a way of life, to a religion — absolutely requires a leap of faith.

Faith is based on what we say we know for sure, but just as much on what we *believe*. What we believe is never sure, it is what we *choose* to hold as true. There is always a risk involved in every choice we make, no greater risk than when we choose what (or who) we are going to believe, and believe in.

The woman who wants to be trouble-free studies the risks, watches the ground for pitfalls in her path, and keeps on thinking. Even the wisest of us, of course, the instant she commits herself to love, accepts the blindfold, and surrenders her rational mind and all her common sense to high-leaping faith: in her beloved, in herself, in her intuition, in her luck — and in her ability to pick herself up, if she has made a mistake, and start again.

Problems exist too deep, dank and dangerous for me, or you, or anyone to tackle without trained help. Rape, incest, child abuse, mental disorders, drug addiction, alcoholism, entrenched eating disorders, criminality and disabling physical conditions all come my way, but their treatment lies beyond my scope. Knowing when it is time to go for expert help and when to encourage a friend or relative to find a therapist is in itself a matter for common sense and intuition. Nevertheless, of every thousand who ask, 'Do I need therapy?' to about nine hundred and ninety it is safe to reply, 'Certainly not!'

Not everyone who writes to the Agony column, by a long shot, needs professional help or would benefit from it. We cannot all help each other all the time; we don't always know how, and helping is not always the most helpful thing to do. Emotions mature, in their way, with patience and solitary exercise, just like muscles or the brain. But a multitude of experts on every little thing hang out their shingles these days and encourage us to be emotionally lazy, so we forget how expert each of us can become by herself, about herself; we forget universal emotional truths and common human responses and we become self-centred and weaker because of it.

Most of us emerge a lot stronger and better off when we get through natural emotional crises, as we must, with the sympathy of friends perhaps, or sometimes with a few words from an agony aunt, but essentially on our own. The fact is there is no way in the world you or I or anyone will ever be able to support a lover or friend or child leaning on us through a rough patch until we ourselves have come through a few of our own on our own two feet.

Many of the women who write in to me are not in the habit of writing letters or putting their thoughts down on paper. One chief good an agony aunt does her readers is to give them a reason to organise their tumultuous, troubled feelings into words. It is simply not possible to write down what you are thinking without starting to make order of your chaos.

I hope this book, by leading you through the processes of problem-solving and the tangential thoughts that go through my mind when I read letters to the Agony column, will encourage you to think your own way through your trouble, or over it, or around it, or, sometimes, under it.

You will find a list of questions at the end of each chapter. They are not for scoring, they will not give you a psychological profile, there are no correct or incorrect answers to any of them: they are there simply to be stepping-stones, to start you dealing beyond the ways we take for granted with the issues raised by problems that may come your way. Their only purpose is to get you thinking, talking, and even writing your thoughts on paper. Words written down give you a grasp of them which you cannot have when they're spoken into air.

Bear in mind, there is no correct answer to any problem: there is the answer you choose and thereafter the ways you choose to make your answer work.

Giving advice is a funny line of work. My ultimate job satisfaction would be for you to do alone what you hope I will do for you when you write to me. Nothing would make this old auntie happier than for all of you to learn at last how to do it yourselves, and put me out of business.

PROBLEM ONE

Where is Mr Wonderful and what's taking him so long?

● ● ● ● ● ● ● ● ● ●

Dear Irma,

I have a successful career in business, a house of my own, a car and a circle of good friends. I have devoted the past ten years, since I was in my early twenties, to building up my career and financial security. Although I have been involved with a few men, I have never been prepared to really invest time and effort in these relationships because of my career. Lately I've started to long to settle down and have a family. I worry there is nobody special in my life. Most of the men I meet are married. I have a very dear companion I've known since we were kids. He's divorced. I can see myself drifting into marriage with him. This is not ideal but the option of being single and childless suddenly terrifies me. Have all my years of hard work been worthwhile? My life seems suddenly empty.

'Unfulfilled'

● ● ● ● ● ● ● ● ● ●

Fulfilment is such an inviting concept, with its cosy overtones of 'ever after' and 'once and for all' and 'no problem'. Completion and permanence — 'fulfilment', in a nutshell — make a comforting idea. And like most easy comfort, the very word 'fulfilment' is totally misleading. For a start, we are capable of so many wonderful achievements, how can any woman expect to complete all she can do, or wants to do, or may discover she wants to do? Even women who have it all don't always have it when they want it, and never have it all at the same time.

The starting point for many problems that come my way, those of other women I mean, must be myself. After all, each of us is her own main area of exploration. Starting from my own experience, I work outwards as fast as I can towards 'Unfulfilled' and others in a similar spot. In my own way and on my own time I've had to learn that unfulfilment is bound to be part of every existence no matter how actively or aggressively it is led.

For instance, for some reason I was never given music lessons as a child, so for half my life an unfulfilled pianist moped around inside me, until one day in my early twenties while listening to others play, I resigned myself once and for all to being a member of the audience. To listen and not play isn't altogether fulfilling, agreed, but it's a whole lot better than nothing.

Come to that, I never found my Mr Wonderful either, though I worked my way through a few candidates, so I suppose an unfulfilled monogamous wife must be rattling around next to the pianist inside me too.

From my experience I know one thing that 'Unfulfilled' cannot yet know, and may never need to know: the failure to hook up with Mr Wonderful is not the worst thing that can happen to a woman, and not the only failure she needs to fear. Finding Mr Wonderful is not the only success a woman can anticipate in life these days. Even imperfect freedom creates untold new possibilities; fulfilment too has become subject to choices and chances that would have astounded grandma.

Of course, no woman dreams, even in her worst nightmares, that she will end up on her own. The ancient fairy tale about the prince and the princess who wakes at last at his kiss has been so soundly drummed into womankind, that it can come as a real surprise to open your eyes one day and find the bed half empty. After the sagging jawline, to accept manlessness in middle age is for some women a final obstacle to be negotiated before achieving relative serenity. For others, it comes as something of a relief to be at last alone in bed.

Although I am heterosexual and have been in my time very keen on it, nothing is perfectly fulfilling. I know now — perhaps I always knew or perhaps I have just come to terms with it — that for me in the long run it was okay to stay single, and, all told, I have no regrets. I'd still rather play honky-tonk blues on a battered upright than second fiddle.

A woman writes, *'Irma, I have so much love to give. I know the man for me is there somewhere. But where is he?'*
I reply, *'He will be wherever you find him . . .'*

Maybe there really is one Mr Wonderful for each Miss Right on earth — one man, one woman, circling the planet like one nut, one bolt, looking to connect in a perfect screw. If this is the case, the chance of their bumping into each other out of so many billions defies calculation.

It is probably because the logical odds are so remote that otherwise rational women can turn superstitious when it comes to love. I have heard from girls who will someday be psychoanalysts, physicists, or computer programmers, but who are ready to listen to stargazers, cosmeticians, fashion designers, and a host of charlatans as long as they advertise or even hint that they know where Mr Wonderful is waiting and how to winkle him out of his hiding-place.

Of course the spells pan out occasionally. Magic is at work every time two people fall in love. And sometimes in every generation first loves last a lifetime at a high pitch of enchantment. But an awful lot of survival depends on making do. Most love affairs outlast the flickering flames of early passion and then survive by the fact of two people knowing they are happier together than not, and deciding to make the very best of the very good thing they have.

A young woman writes, *'He's eighteen and I'm sixteen. How can I make my parents understand that we are in love for ever? I will never find any other man for me . . .'*
I reply, *'Never mind "for ever". "For ever" will take care of itself. Love him for another six months; that should begin to help persuade your parents . . .'*

Candidly, I'd rather receive a hundred letters from 'Unfulfilleds' looking for Mr Wonderful in their early thirties than just one from a sixteen- or seventeen-year-old who imagines she has found him. Every living thing changes. Healthy youthful change means growing and sometimes outgrowing. What fulfils today can become merely satisfying later, and later still can turn into a major pain in the proverbial. And whenever a girl traps herself in a hasty commitment to what feels like fulfilment at seventeen, eighteen, nineteen, it's a decision that will seriously stunt her growth.

Today's fulfilment is hardly ever enough for tomorrow's needs, which is the main reason why it is utter folly at any age to look for all fulfilment from a man, or children, or any other human being. Besides, responsibility for *your* fulfilment is an unfair, unloving burden to put on others who may still be searching for fulfilment of their own. 'Fulfilment' can be sought with a lover, sure, and sometimes found with him, but it's childish and downright nuts to expect it *from* a lover.

Nowadays, by the way, women writing to the Agony column refer to their lovers fashionably as 'partners'. 'Partner' sounds more worthy and serious than 'lover', doesn't it? More grown-up, and feet on the ground. But it all boils down to the same thing in the end: let a woman call him her lover or partner or husband or merely her friend, chances are she still expects the poor sap to do everything she thinks he should, and take responsibility for her happiness.

'Unfulfilled' could more accurately have signed her letter 'Unhappy'. Happiness is of course what practically everyone means to say when they refer to 'fulfilment'. But fulfilment and happiness are not the same thing. The most fulfilled people in the end are those who have worked the hardest and given more than they've received: they have probably not led lives of ordinary happiness, nor necessarily been very happy at all.

At least 'Unfulfilled' acknowledges that love affairs require an investment of 'time and effort' once past the early stage, and she doesn't kid herself that fulfilment will be as easy as falling off a log. When agony aunts and other busybodies like me go on and on about how you have to 'work at a relationship', what we mean is that fulfilment cannot exist without challenge: love is no end in itself, in other words. Love is easy. Love is only the overture to an adventure: endeavour and compromise and fulfilment come later.

I must say that not even at the most unhappy points in my life, not even at the end of my first serious love affair when I was alone and crushed a long time ago in Paris, would I have signed a letter 'Un-fulfilled'. 'Unhappy', yes. But 'Unfulfilled'? It sounds too redolent of regret. And in the main, *je ne regrette rien*.

Somehow, while I deliver my down-to-earth advice about man-hunting, I will have to discourage 'Unfulfilled' from the temptation to regret that she already hints at in her letter. The life 'Unfulfilled' led felt right at the time, it *was* right at the time, and if she had life to live again, she would lead it precisely the same way. So would you. So would I. And knowing no more than we knew, so would every last one of us. Regret is of less than no use at all: it keeps a woman's head swivelled around looking back at the path she has already travelled, judging today what was done yesterday, so busy passing sentence on herself in retrospect, she will keep tripping over her own feet.

'Unfulfilled' set her own high standards and did a good job of achieving them: house, job, income, friends. Now unfamiliar urges are begging for satisfaction. She wants a man. Maybe she'll find one, maybe she won't: the next stage of her fulfilment, like the earlier one, is up to her.

Poor 'Unfulfilled'. All she wanted when she wrote to me was in-structions on how to get a man, and here am I lost in a lecture on the meaning of fulfilment. Hardly a word of all this will figure in my printed answer, by the way, and if 'Unfulfilled' were right here sit-ting in front of me, I probably wouldn't bother her with all this abstract stuff. However, any help anyone can give herself or anyone else must be built on a foundation of what she holds in general to be true. If I did not mull over 'Unfulfilled's' problem and let my thoughts loose off the lead, I could as well send 'Unfulfilled' a list of dating agencies.

By all means, let us be practical about what ails us, but always bearing in mind that practical answers without imagination are rather like a telephone directory: useful, sure, but not very gripping to read, and no fun at all to write. I cannot give 'Unfulfilled' a meta-phorical pat on the head and assure her that nothing is easier than for a mature woman who is successful in her career to run out and grab a mate for making babies. I wish it weren't so, but anyone with the least power of observation who is not fuddled by wishful thinking or distracted by what she thinks *should* be, must notice that the serious pursuit of worldly success *does* affect a woman's marital status, you bet your bottom drawer it does.

I didn't make the rules, and far be it from me to discourage a young woman from pursuing a serious career if that is what she has a mind to do, but don't let her imagine Harrison Ford clones are hanging around looking to get laid in the executive suite. If the truth of the matter discourages any young woman from aiming for the top at her work, then it is as well if she *does* think twice about a competitive career where singlemindedness is the key to success and Mr Wonderful can end up being the ultimate luxury item.

Besides, office romances deserve a chapter of their own: when they do occur, they can drag along malicious gossip, envy, tainted office politics, and a whole mass of problems peculiarly their own.

As 'Unfulfilled' and ambitious women like her climb the professional ladder they have a natural tendency, sensible or not, to look at men on their own rung or above it for possible dates. The higher a woman looks for a man, the fewer men there are, and the more likely those few will already be married, as 'Unfulfilled' has discovered. Or dating bimbos. Or both.

I know this all sounds negative. And if the agony aunt must err towards any bias, optimism is the more constructive — *realistic* optimism. Nobody can afford to be negative when she is looking for solutions, but even less can she afford to be dishonest, with herself or anyone else. So let's be honest and tell it like it is. Honestly, there are a lot fewer 'New Men' around than newish men or slightly used men, and when a woman's job status or salary touches his own or tops it, the ordinary man of any age feels threatened to some degree by her, even if he thinks he shouldn't. Threatened men make lousy lovers.

Mind you, not all that many women, even liberated women, feel comfortable on top; some are uncomfortable as equals too, even when they believe they should be equal. At least 'Unfulfilled' sounds comfortable enough on that score, and even though she's successful, independent and well off, she has a way to go before she needs to take her vows of chastity. There are still plenty of chances to attract Mr Wonderful and sign him up for life.

Women like 'Unfulfilled', organised women who are ambitious and busy at work, have been steadily concentrating their spheres of activity and streamlining their address books. I'll bet if I could ask her, she would say she feels as if she has already met all the friends she will have in her lifetime.

18

'I used to think that too,' I'd say to her. 'But then I learned that we never reach the limit of our friendships, not until we have reached the limit of ourselves.'

The fact is, 'Unfulfilled' is in a rut, and Mr Wonderfuls hardly ever tumble into ruts.

It's a tiny, irritating mystery that Mr Wonderful often turns up precisely when a girl is not looking for him, and even when she has good reasons to wish he'd keep his distance. Why should this be? I think it's because women actively seeking love grow desperate, and desperation is not sexy. The instant a man senses that a woman is desperate, she's in trouble. Desperation is unflattering both to her, and to the guy she sets her sights on: it suggests she can't do better than him and that immediately makes him think he couldn't do worse than her. A mere sniff of the hungry hunting woman's desperation and off leaps the proud, nervous buck to fields safe and new.

By the same token, males in general tend to find attractive she who is otherwise engaged. Thus, when what you are really seeking is a mate (or just a date) it's not a bad idea to seek something else altogether. What should that something be? Something you have truly wondered about or always wanted to try, something that will lead you into new, unexplored areas of your own resources, something you can undertake with genuine enthusiasm. Enthusiasm is madly sexy. Enthusiasm brightens the eye and puts spring in the step. Enthusiasm attracts.

A woman writes, *'I have joined everything from sky-diving clubs to bridge clubs . . . I've tried it all, just like you advised. Why haven't I met Mr Wonderful . . .?'*
I reply, *'I never said to try it all, only what you want to try . . .'*

Enthusiasm has to be real — it is harder to fake than orgasm. And why try to fake it? What would be the point, say, for 'Unfulfilled' to pretend she's dying to shoot pool if it's really because she figures a pool hall is a good place to meet men? A pool hall is a good place to meet pool-players, just as mid-air is where you meet sky divers, and a bridge club is where you go to have your high hopes trumped. If 'Unfulfilled' isn't genuinely interested in, say, pool, any guy who is interested in the game will take one look and spot her right off for a phoney. I'm not saying she won't get it on with him; having sniffed a fake, he might take what's on offer. Why not? But chances are slim he will take it seriously.

Everything we do pulls along a lot of by-products, and whatever 'Unfulfilled' goes into, be it athletic, musical, intellectual, recreational, artistic, or just something fun she has always had in the back of her mind to give a whirl, if she undertakes it with real enthusiasm and curiosity, is bound to broaden her outlook, extend her confidence, introduce her to likeminded people, and add to her knowledge. So what if Mr Wonderful does not surface? Even if he never appears on the scene, she will have enriched her life significantly. Can that be bad?

Whenever I read a letter or listen to the sorrow of a friend, I am bound to remember hundreds of similar problems, yet every one of them is different, because each is from a woman with her own handwriting, her own turn of phrase, her own taste in stationery, sometimes even a trace of perfume on the page: a unique set of references all her own that gives intuition some clues to her special nature.

All problem-solving is to some extent a process of elimination, and for a moment while reading 'Unfulfilled's' letter, my mind wandered to all the women I hear from who do not have freedom even to pursue the possibility of fulfilment: a small but important group, young and not so young, trapped at home with aged or disabled parents.

A woman writes, *'I am thirty years old. I was the only child of older parents who kept me their "little girl". My father died when I was in my teens and I live with my mother who is blind. I have never had a sexual relationship . . . I have no girlfriends . . . if I go anywhere, it is with my mother . . .'*

It's a fact that some women (and men) find peace in a life of service and obedience, but contented people do not write to an agony aunt. 'Is it too late for me?' the unhappy ones ask. It is not early, nor is it late, I tell them: it is time to grab their lives and make a break for it. Of course, I recommend they plan their escapes thoroughly and see to it their dependants receive all the assistance they can afford or that our society offers. I can't kid myself it will be easy for them, nowhere near as easy as it is for me to sit in comfort and dole out advice. And I can never forget that they are the ones who must find the courage to resist their fate — long after I have moved on to other letters, they alone will suffer the aftermath of their decision.

Lucky 'Unfulfilled', she has her house, her position, her friends: 'Unfulfilled' is free to do whatever she must and go wherever she can to seek anything she dreams will be fulfilling. There is always a mean-spirited temptation in me to remind her of others less fortunate who have no access to opportunities, and not much chance at all of finding any sort of fulfilment, let alone of tracking down a Mr Wonderful. But nobody's tears have ever evaporated because someone else is shedding more of them and faster.

Except sometimes in cases of illness or physical handicap, it never helps in the slightest to point out others who are worse off than the person who is asking for your help.

Can any young girl today believe that it used to be commonly held that a woman out for a man was smart to keep away from other women? Particularly if the other women were on the loose, too. Way back then, most young women met their future mates through their families and family friends. These days, when it comes to Mr Wonderful, an independent woman like 'Unfulfilled', long since out of the nest, is going to have to go out there and track him down by herself.

'Unfulfilled' has good friends; she refers to them in her letter, and some of them are probably single women who are also in the market for mates. They could do a lot worse than pool their resources. Two or three women can boldly go where a woman on her own feels out of place: to clubs, restaurants, bars, concerts, or to holiday resorts. Men are timid creatures too, believe it or not, and fearful of rejection, though they try not to show it. A lot of nice guys find it easier to approach a pair of women or a group in a public place. A single woman is an unknown quantity to a man — she could be waiting for someone else; she could be desperate, hungry, dangerous. How does he know he isn't misreading her signals?

Although I can't pretend that friendships between females do not engender monumental problems of their own which account for about ten per cent of my postbag (and have accounted for a similar percentage of the misery in my own life), still, and all the company of women is absolutely fabulous. Contrary to popular opinion, women together have very little smalltalk. In no time even women who have never met before will be deep into an intense, meaningful, up-roarious conversation about their own lives and life in general which only the envious — men, usually — dismiss as 'gossip'.

Women on the same wavelength when they go out on the town to-gether always end up having a good time. Only a nincompoop would consider a jolly night out with the girls a waste of time because she failed to pick up Mr Wonderful. Younger women than 'Unful-filled' generally go only to bars and clubs in search of Mr Wonderful. Because time stood still during their marriages and that is where they used to go, so do newly divorced women.

A woman writes, *'Aren't there any real men left? I go out clubbing with my girlfriends, and every guy we meet just wants sex. I hate the whole idea of the one night stand, but that's all there is out there . . .'*

If the men you meet in bars and clubs only want sex, well then, why not hunt in new territory? Be imaginative. Stretch your resources. In-vest in a good time. Concerts, movies, shopping, new jobs, new cities, Mexico, parks, malls, libraries, PTA meetings, drag racing, Canada, renewing old friendships, white-water rafting, theatres, volunteer work, TV shows, Alaska: the world is full of places new to you, and some of them are just around the corner. I can't tell you or anyone exactly where to look for her Mr Wonderful. However, if you want a lover with staying power beyond breakfast in bed, then I can tell you where *not* to go: do not follow the lemmings to watering-holes where music and booze and friction all conspire towards a one night stand.

A friend of mine from India often tells me how she thinks 'Un-fulfilled' and the rest of us are frantic and deluded in our search for Mr Wonderful. Her marriage was arranged for her by her parents. 'Tell me who knows me as well as they do, Irma, or could so much want the best for me?' They nominated numerous suitable young men for her to meet until they finally found one she liked the look of, and in due course she decided she could happily set up house with him and make a life. 'If a man and a woman are both compatible decent people, why should marriage not come first,' she asks, 'and love come afterwards?'

My friend, by the way, practises law, has been happily married now for ten years, and has two children. I am delighted for her. But I'm afraid I cannot recommend to 'Unfulfilled' that she run right home and ask her parents to help her find a mate. Rebelliousness has become a stage of adolescence in the West as predictable as acne. Our lives move so much more quickly here and now than in ages and places less technologically driven; information is spread with incredible speed; new fashions and forms of expression spring up and are broadcast practically overnight: youth is constantly redesigning itself, leaving older members of the family behind, so it is no wonder familial ties have stretched and loosened.

In our society parents do not necessarily know their grown daughters much better than friends or colleagues do: often they know them less well. Anyhow, 'Unfulfilled' is heir to the great western romantic tradition. My Indian friend rather sorrowfully admits that in the cities of her homeland women, and men too, have been seduced by the Hollywood ethic: these days each wants to find her own Mr Wonderful in a blaze of glory, the way it happens in the movies, thank you very much. And they have begun to resist arranged marriages. She doubts whether her own daughter, who has been raised in New York, will consent to one.

As for marriage-brokers, they still function in many parts of the world, though around here they are something of a joke. I would not seriously send 'Unfulfilled' to a marriage-broker, assuming I knew where one was to be found. Marriage-brokers are as out of date as that worn old pick-up line, 'Hey! Capricorn is, like, my affinity . . .' Arranged marriage, often based on astrological compatibility, has no role left in a society like ours that interprets freedom as a bewildering multitude of personal choices.

But, having dismissed all the traditional aids to love, what is wrong with online courtship, specialised advertising and dating agencies? They are nothing more and not much less than modern enactments of the ancient matchmaking traditions. Probably because both sexes go into to it separately yet together, desperation does not have to attach itself to people who subscribe to dating agencies, and such like.

Unfortunately, we women especially tend to lose our critical faculties the instant we encounter the merest hope of romance. All that is remotely wrong or dangerous about high-tech matchmaking are the unreal expectations of those who apply for it.

Is it safe to trust that 'Unfulfilled's' business acumen indicates a cool head? I hope so. There is nothing an agony aunt likes more than a general rule, and as a general rule our actions count not for their aims alone, but also for the manner in which we undertake them. The way you do things matters, in other words, every bit as much as why you do them. If 'Unfulfilled' decides to go public in her search for Mr Wonderful, I hope her attitude will be upfront, so it makes the whole experiment bold and stylish and amusing without in the least detracting from her genuine intent, which is to find Mr Wonderful. If 'Unfulfilled' decides to have recourse to techno-dating, she will need to see it in her own mind not as a last resort, but as the choice of a grown woman who is too busy for all the rules of the old dating game, and who wants to try to cut through all the crap. Otherwise, if she goes in embarrassed and dizzily hopeful, she will be self-conscious and fearful, and bound for disappointment.

Whenever women are polled about what they want in a lover, sense of humour figures high on the list. We women have a sense of humour too. Must we lose it absolutely every time the subject is love? If 'Unfulfilled' keeps in touch with her sense of humour, it will see her through, like the balancing stick of a tightrope walker. Who knows? With luck she could find a guy who has gone into arranged or on-line romance with the same cheerful, not overly solemn, attitude.

Has there ever been a friend or a lover who was not first a stranger? I have always been a great believer in talking to strangers. But I find myself hesitating to recommend it to lonely women. What stops me is not that life has become more dangerous — life has always been dangerous, it's just that never before have so many warnings been posted all over the place — but it is my impression that, especially in America, women are losing confidence in that combination of observation, common sense and instinct known widely as our intuition. In other words, we no longer trust ourselves to get ourselves out of sticky situations, particularly if they involve a predatory man; we cry for help more often and sooner, because we are forgetting how to help ourselves.

'Dear Irma,

   I think I was date-raped last night . . . I was drunk . . . does that count?' (Whatever happened to self-preservation?)

'He takes drugs in a big way . . . don't tell me to leave him, Irma, because I love him . . .' (Whatever happened to common sense?)

'I used to love my job but my boss made a suggestive remark to me and I'm so upset, I want to quit . . .' (Whatever happened to dignity and a sense of proportion?)

Wouldn't it be a shame — and more, a *disaster* — if we allowed the light of our emergent equality to dim our old survival techniques. For instance, there can be no woman born (and in charge of all her faculties) who cannot handle the unwelcome attentions of a raunchy male without running to a court of law, or going into nervous collapse, or joining a victims' help group.

'I would only enrol with a dating agency,' the twenty-two-year-old daughter of a New York friend said to me, 'if they had on record how many times the guy had said "I love you", and to how many different women. If he'd said it a lot, I wouldn't bother to meet him.'

'In that case,' I replied, 'how would you ever know whether, when he said it to you, it wasn't the first time he ever meant it?'

No life can be without risks, not if it is worth living. Coping with risk is up to each and every one of us. The law and other authorities are increasingly on our side, as they exist to be equally on the side of every citizen, but in the end, if a woman doesn't know she can take care of herself, she is more helpless and dependent on Big Daddy than ever.

Yes, there are lunatics and villains who slip past even the most stringent vetting. But I trust 'Unfulfilled' is not so completely brainwashed by 'experts' and out of touch with her instincts that she won't recognise a lothario or a weirdo practically on sight, and know how to give the guy the elbow.

Terrible things happen. They always have. But wonderful things happen too. And nothing at all happens to a girl without the guts to take calculated risks. So meet strange men in brightly lit places with a crowd of other people nearby, and try to remember the gift of intuition that kept all us women safe long, long before sexual harassment and date rape became high-fashion squawks.

A woman writes, *'Where is a Kevin Costner for me?'*
I reply, *'There is no "a Kevin Costner". There is only the Kevin Costner. And he's a very busy man.'*

What does the girl in search of 'her' Kevin Costner know about him?

Absolutely nothing except that in his movies he's cute in a sort of big-brotherly way, if you like the type.

Some of the requirements that come my way for Mr Wonderful are superficial and really very silly. Smoking, for example, has become a moral issue: smokers are 'bad', non-smokers are 'good'. Now, I don't much like cigarette smoke any more myself, especially first thing in the morning. Tobacco is an irritant, yes, but it is not a mind-altering drug, nor does it make smokers violent, sly or evil. It astounds me that anybody could seriously consider a weakness for tobacco reason enough not to love another human being, even to despise him. And it gets worse.

How petty and self-centred do we intend to become in our time? 'You women,' said a smallish man I know after he'd enrolled in a dating agency, 'you are all "heightist".' Show me, please, where it is written that the male of any couple must be the taller? Only in every other small ad placed by a woman in search of her Mr Wonderful. Even on the brink of desperation, most women still cannot imagine being taller than their dates or mates.

A woman writes, *'I am twenty-three, have a good job and am attractive and intelligent. But I can't find a partner. Every man I meet is either not goodlooking enough, rich enough or intelligent enough. Am I looking for an ideal that just doesn't exist?'*
I reply, *'Good looks change. Poor men become rich. Rich men lose their money. Intelligence lasts, yes, but we can appreciate it in others only according to how much of it we possess ourselves. What I believe you are actually telling me is that you are twenty-three years old and you have not yet fallen madly in love. When it happens, it could be with a poor man who is quite plain and hasn't got a lot to say for himself, but somehow he manages to make your heart turn cartwheels. God alone knows why . . .'*

Another woman writes, *'I am twenty-two. All I want is to get married and have children, and be in love and be loved by someone for ever . . .'*
I reply, *'Is that all you want? How about a really big lottery win while you're at it, or a magic carpet . . . ?'*

Nobody ought to settle for less than she knows she needs from a relationship, not on any score, and I defy anyone to persuade me it is not better to be single for ever than disastrously hitched. Nevertheless, juvenile criteria for Mr Wonderful can be mercifully relaxed with time and even dropped altogether with no loss whatsoever to his sensitivity, sense of humour, fidelity, honesty, and similar key qualities that come up in the list all the time whenever a woman is asked to describe her ideal man.

One real advantage 'Unfulfilled' has in looking for a mate in her maturity instead of earlier on is that she has no doubt abandoned most of the trivial adornments of her dream man. But even after his taste in clothes, cars and furniture has ceased to matter, and the colour of his eyes, his height, how much hair he has on his chest no longer concern her, even after 'Unfulfilled' is ready to accept a bumpy marital history, perhaps children from a previous union, possibly a clinging ex-wife, and similar flaws in her yet-to-be-found Mr Wonderful, there remain requirements of race, religion, social standing, age, education and income: to what degree are they a fixed, integral part of her ideal man? Or anyone's?

A woman writes, *'I'm twenty-one and I've been dating my boyfriend for seven months now. What bothers me is the way people talk about us and look at us when we're together. He is black and I am white. My mother can't stand it . . . and doesn't want anything to do with me. I fear I will ultimately have to choose between my boyfriend and my parents. I love my boyfriend very much. What should I do?'*

Romance between people of different races has special problems, of course it has, and the odds increase against winning any gamble for happiness, mostly because of the pressure of outside opinion, but also because it is harder to read signals across chasms of culture or time or upbringing, and easier to misread needs. Just talk to any mother, for instance, who has tried to get her child back from an absconding Islamic husband, and ask her what she imagined her marriage to him was going to be like when she was in the first flush of love. Then ask her to tell you how the facts compare to her romantic dream? And ask him, come to that, what made him think his western bride understood his very different tradition and would be able to conform to it?

Mind you, 'Unfulfilled's' sophisticated business friends and her parents, who are no doubt more desperate even than she for her to marry, would probably accept an inter-racial affair with a man of the right status and age faster than if she were to come up with, say, a nineteen-year-old, bisexual, out-of-work actor and present him to everyone as the man of her life.

Believe me, if an adult professional woman like 'Unfulfilled' wrote to me from the edge of commitment to an underage, sexually ambiguous, underemployed Romeo I'd probably lace into her too. So what? In the end, she and she alone decides exactly how and why her chosen Mr Wonderful satisfies essential needs. And when she believes herself to be as sure as she can be, then it has to be to hell with me, or anyone else who claims to know better. When it all goes wrong later, she can hardly blame *him* for being what he had to be, and what she was too besotted to notice he was all along. And she can hardly blame me, or anyone who tried to warn her. If she must blame anything, she can only blame love and chemistry. And then, with no regrets and some jolly memories, I hope she will in due course be free of the need to repeat the experience.

Nobody is more vulnerable to future humiliation than a woman who makes a romantic choice against the advice of people who mean her well. By the same token, nobody is more despicable than a well-wisher who later says 'I told you so.' Besides, I've begun to wonder if it is not necessary to the continuation of our species that a few of us are always in the process of making fools of ourselves for love. They deserve our gratitude, these martyrs to romance, though it costs them all their peace on earth, for they keep banners flying on the flagships of our novelists and poets. Perhaps there is even a natural imperative for crazy illogical coupling now and again, to keep the gene pool perky.

A woman writes, *'Dear Irma, please help! There's this gorgeous guy hanging around under my balcony. But our families are deadly enemies and will oppose the irrepressible love we feel for each other. I am only fourteen, but mature for my age . . .'*
I reply, *'Dear Juliet, I'm sure you're over-dramatising the way teenagers always do . . .'*

An agony aunt need never fear that her common-sense advice will dissuade mad lovers from their grand and tragic destiny: mad lovers may consult apothecaries, stargazers and witches, but not even the craziest of them would have recourse to an agony aunt.

When it comes to disparities in the human condition, I have little trouble with racial differences, but some of the young women who write to me have trouble with them, and in a way they do not want to see or realise.

A woman writes, *'I am a black single parent . . . at first everything was great between me and my white boyfriend, but communication between us is failing . . . I am starting to think he only moved in with me as a way of rebelling against his rich family . . .'*
I reply, *'I salute your courage . . .'*

In a postbag full of daydreams, any letter from a writer who actually faces an unflattering possibility, and analyses it, earns an agony aunt's respect. She's a woman I'd have next to me in the trenches. I'd like so much to be able to assure her she is wrong to think her lover is using their inter-racial love affair to score a political point. But how can I? The chances are he is. Some of the girls who write to me in outraged righteousness about parental disapproval have chosen a Mr Wonderful their family must find unsuitable precisely in order to sock one in the eye to mummy or daddy. Why should a man not be capable of equally childish and selfish behaviour? Of course, just because the guy is selfish and childish does not exactly mean he doesn't love her. If love required lovers to be perfect gentlemen, or even to be bright, very little loving would get off the ground.

Unfashionable though it is to say so these days, great age difference can also be a real block to long-term happiness. Of course it can. A younger man who chooses an older woman is practically by definition on some level bone-lazy. Just look at all the ageing celebrities who make the proven error of waltzing off with toyboys who sooner or later take them for a ride? Only a lazy guy would be willing and eager to settle into a ready-made life based on *her* success, *her* family, and a comfortable future that has cost him no personal effort or ambition beyond his pectorals.

And a girl who falls for a much older man really is looking not for grown-up love at all, but for a daddy, like it says in the books, or a sugar daddy. In either case it will probably be a love she is very likely one day to outgrow or discard. Yes, yes, I know there are lots of exceptions, but for every Oona O'Neill and Charlie Chaplin there are a heap of unions that did not make it across the generation gap.

Fortunately, what once may have seemed a vast age difference of, say, nine or ten years when it was the man who was the younger of the two, or eighteen or twenty years when he was the older partner, no longer matters as much, now that youth has become a more elastic concept.

A woman writes, *'I met my beloved at university, but now we've graduated our differences are becoming apparent. I'm from a working-class background. I'm egalitarian, humanist and want to right all the world's wrongs. He comes from a wealthy middle-class family. His mother is the biggest snob I know. The physical attraction is explosive, we can't bear to be apart. He isn't a snob, but I could never be the wife he'll need to cook dinner parties and arrange flowers in a St Laurent dress all day. I suppose we'll have to split up some day . . .'*

I reply, *'Does he agree with your humanitarian world-vision? If he does not and you are truly committed to your principles, then your union will be in trouble after the sexual fire dies down. Otherwise, all people in love have to come to terms with something. Your beloved is not a snob, you say. Are you a snob? Do you think because he comes from a rich home he cannot be your equal in sensitivity or understanding? That's an odd kind of egalitarianism.'*

Whether the difference between a woman and her candidate for Mr Wonderful is in age, race, or social standing, she will take flak for it from outsiders (from his side if his social standing is higher, from her side if it is lower). Marriage, or any formal union between a man and a woman, is a social contract, after all, and when people say, 'You could have done better,' they actually mean that she is letting the side down. They are snobs, in other words, and their opinions have no more wisdom than dropped names or bubbles.

Granted, it sounds weaselly to say so, but the honest truth must be that when a woman needs to ask me what to do about reconciling her love with her family or her community, then it suggests she is not as settled in her choice as she hopes. And if anything I have to say helps her decide to give up her lover, then in the end public opinion matters more to her than him, and he just wasn't Mr Wonderful enough. Which is fair enough. Why not? Social and parental ties do matter in this life, to some of us more than to others, and sometimes they are bound to outweigh romantic love: ask any royal prince or princess.

Each of us has to decide for herself somewhere along the line which of the cards she was dealt at birth she wants to hold on to and which she thinks it is safe to throw away. Every generation believes it knows better than the one before, and so it does — about passing fears and today's short-term ambitions — however, certain truths remain and in one form or another will outlive fashion. Among the perennials is the corny, homegrown fact that what a person searches for far and wide is sometimes, not always, right there under her uppity nose.

A woman writes, *'Dear Irma, I am falling in love with my co-worker. He doesn't know. We are really good friends and there are times I think he might feel the same way about me. I'm afraid to spoil our friendship. Do I have to leave my job?'*

I reply, *'Desire makes heat and it shows first in the eyes. Look him in the eye, think heat, feel heat, transmit heat, and if he doesn't get the message, he's probably a dud.'*

A while ago I met a woman from Boston who made her living going around America giving courses in flirtation — a bit like teaching breathing, I would have hoped, and not a career I ever envisaged for myself. But practically every postbag brings in letters from women attracted sexually to men who see themselves as friends, no more, no less. They say they are afraid to ruin the friendship by making a sexual overture. It is quite correct that sexual intercourse is not exactly a friendly act. But for crying out loud, unless the guy is married, or she is, or he is gay, or he is seriously depraved, what is she waiting for? Are we losing our ancient gifts to such a degree that we no longer know ways to show sexual interest more subtle than to throw a guy to the ground and grab his crotch?

As for quitting a job if an awkward pass goes wrong with a co-worker, is the girl off her trolley? It all blows over in less time than it takes to tell, and besides, these days another job can be a whole lot harder to find than another man.

'Unfulfilled' says the option of being single and childless scares her, but there is an even more scary option. Neither marriage nor even a stable union is absolutely necessary to the production of offspring: babies can be made without benefit of wedlock — I have a wonderful twenty-two-year-old son who proves that basic fact of life. Motherhood, organised and independent and self-financed, was the greatest adventure of my existence.

Take my word for it, to have been born of an unwed, unattached mother does not have to mean a baby was unplanned: I may have

31

thrown in most of the cards I was dealt, but I have never been careless of human life, not my own and certainly not that of a child I pledged to love and raise. For me, and some others left out of the feminists' equations and scorned by traditionalists, the maternal drive is not cute or cosy or warm; it is raging, fierce, and so hungry it was going to eat me alive had I not found a way to appease it in time.

A woman writes, *'My last date was over two years ago. I'm scared of being alone and childless for the rest of my miserable life. I plan on finding a man to make me pregnant by my twenty-fourth bithday next year, or killing myself . . .'*

Not in a million years will I ever suggest to 'Unfulfilled', or anyone, that she do as I did in my late thirties — throw in the towel on Mr Wonderful, and go it alone into self-sufficient motherhood. To raise healthy happy children with help is hard enough; to raise them on your own is the hardest job in the world. It worked for me because I worked my tail off to make it work. And it was a well-planned decision that brought me nothing but joy. But what if hysterics who threaten life or death by age twenty-four and similarly excitable girls were to read my words as encouragement to spawn alone and heedlessly?

Too many young women in their twenties, or even younger, upon feeling maternal stirrings for the first time are so astounded and impatient that they do not stop to consider how little they alone have to offer a baby, and how many years they have in hand. Youth lasts a long time nowadays, yet it is more dangerously impatient than ever.

'Unfulfilled' has time to make up her mind about a lot of things. Maybe her Mr Wonderful will never make an appearance, and maybe she will be driven by a maternal urge as overwhelming as my own to a solution as extreme as mine. If she does decide to have a baby on her own, and I get wind of it, I'll support her to the limit, but she'll have to get there without any urging from me, or anyone else.

Then again, if her biological clock is not set to explode but only, as many do, to tick-tock to a gentle halt, and if she never finds Mr Wonderful, or even just a comfortable match, then her potential for love, deprived of traditional objects, can be fulfilled in countless other ways that help to make this world a better place, as the generosity and energy and love of childless and single women have always done.

• • • • • • • • • •

Dear 'Unfulfilled',

Bring to bear on the problem of finding your Mr Wonderful all the qualities that have made you successful in your business life: imagination, high but realistic goals, ambition, organisational and communicative skills. In what areas can you open up new markets for personal expansion? Be creative about your extra-curricular activities: from all the things you've ever wanted to try to learn or do, choose one that is slightly off-beat so it leads you into groups of people outside your own profession and line of work. Then, why not plan a holiday in a new place off the beaten track? In your position, I'd travel alone (in my position I'd travel alone; I like to travel alone), but if you can't see your way clear to that, choose your companions very, very carefully. The point is to shake up your non-working life and let the pieces fall in brand new patterns.

Advertise yourself if you have a mind to do it. Maybe some great guy out there has signed up for a dating agency or reads small ads in the same spirit of what-the-hell as you. The search for a soulmate is an investment of self and, if you must look back, then do it with pride in all you have accomplished and made of yourself: your very own, one-and-only, genuine, one-hundred-per-cent self. All your achievements have turned you into a prize for any Mr Wonderful: would you want a man without the wit to know how good you are?

Do not panic. A woman in panic does not 'drift' into the wrong relationships; she leaps into them, or falls into them, or hops into them like a headless chicken. And while we are on the topic, that dear companion you've known since childhood? Try looking at him as if you'd just been introduced. Sensible women want to fall

madly in love and then hope love will turn into abiding friendship:
why should it not be just as smart, even smarter, to arrange things
the other way around?

Hopefully,
Aunt Irma

● ● ● ● ● ● ● ● ● ●

AGONY AUNT'S WORKSHEET

1. Do you believe there is just one Mr Wonderful for every woman?
2. Is believing the same as knowing?
3. Do you *believe* there is one man for one woman in this life, or do you *know* it?
4. Do you *believe* there is one man for one woman, or do you *hope* so?
5. Even if you think age difference doesn't matter, list three reasons it could matter.
6. What are the attributes of your Mr Wonderful, starting with the *least* important?
7. Name something and someone you found fulfilling ten years ago. Do they fulfil you now?
8. How would you reply to 'Unfulfilled's' letter?

PROBLEM TWO

What is commitment and how do I get it?

●●●●●●●●●●

Dear Irma,

Three years ago I met my boyfriend. We got engaged but decided to wait before getting married. I am now twenty-three. We bought a house together over a year ago, and I recently brought up the subject of commitment. He said he no longer wanted to marry me; he still loves me, but he doesn't ever want to get married and I shouldn't take it personally. I feel let down and cheated. I am not prepared to stick around without security or commitment. I love him, but I don't think I can stay, knowing he will never commit himself. The more I try to think things out, the more in a muddle I am.

'Confused'

●●●●●●●●●●

Commitment is a relatively new word in the lexicon of emotional agony. It began to crackle out of my morning postbag in the hard-hearted eighties, as I recall. Until then it had been applied to religion and politics more commonly than to personal and romantic attachments: a man was more likely to be a 'committed Democrat', say, or a 'committed Christian' than a committed lover. For that matter, he was more likely to be committed to an institution such as prison or a psychiatric ward than to the institution of marriage.

Odd, isn't it? We commit suicide, we commit murder, we commit capital crimes all too frequently, but we still do not say 'they committed marriage'. Yet what is the commitment that 'Confused' and thousands like her want from their man in the end? The commitment of good old wedlock, that's what. Of course, there are stages of commitment, I guess, from 'pick you up at eight' through 'I love you' to what used to be called an 'engagement', more likely now to be living together with a 'partner', but they still don't count for much unless they culminate in 'I do'.

Commitment is in fact another of the partnerish, significant-otherish, relationshipish, feeling-good-about-myselfish words we choose to use because they are more self-contained and less emotive than the tender old words (lover, love affair, happy) and so we try to give the utterly deluded impression of being in control of love and other unexpected feelings, and of ourselves. 'Love' itself has been discarded in some politically correct circles, to be replaced by 'care', as in 'I care for you', so much less alarming and yielding, and so much more self-centred than the abandoned old feeling that's responsible for most of our trouble.

Why won't he commit himself? As often as I am asked that question, I imagine a dialogue in my mind with the girl:

She: 'Why won't he commit himself?'
Me: 'Why should he commit himself?'
She: 'Because I'm ready for commitment.'
Me: 'What if he isn't ready?'
She: 'If he really loved me, he would be.'
Me: 'Are you saying he doesn't love you?'
She: 'I know he loves me. Why won't he commit himself?'
Me: 'Why should he commit himself?'
She: 'Because I'm ready for it . . .'

Judging by my postbag, young men do not appear to be as persuaded as young women that commitment is necessarily a fair expression of love, or even of 'caring'. Love and marriage do not, in other words, go together in the male mind like a horse and carriage. Readiness rather than love seems to generate commitment as far as men are concerned, the moment rather than generalised hormonal zest for nesting, timing more than emotion. When they are afraid of marriage it is not necessarily because they still want to play the field, though that can be a part of it; more likely it's because they are not yet ready to be as they see their fathers: responsible, worn down, ageing and dull.

A woman writes, *'He says he doesn't want to marry me and never will marry anyone. I only want him. Should I expect him to be more sensitive to my needs?'*
I reply, *'Want whatever you must, and dream on, but what good will it do to expect him to be other than he is . . .?'*

A lot of young men see formal commitment, even to a woman they dearly love, even to one with whom they are already sharing a roof, as a surrender and the beginning of the end of the good times. And as long as a man does not yet envision marriage as a happy next step, then he is quite simply not yet ready. Perhaps he will never be.

A woman writes, *'My boyfriend is refusing to have sex with me. He says he is not ready for commitment. He says he doesn't mind my kissing him but when I do, he's not exactly enthusiastic in return. Friends say he's just using me . . .'*
I reply, *'What do your friends say he is using you for? He is not your boyfriend. A boyfriend is a man who, when you kiss him, does more than just tolerate it. He seems to reject what you offer. And what you offer essentially is commitment. He doesn't want it . . .'*

As often as not, a woman believes that as soon as a man is married he will change from a bad boy into a polite one, from a drunk, say, into a teetotaller, from a flirt into someone with eyes for her alone, from a playboy into a provider. As often as not, a young man believes that if he marries the sweet girl he loves, she will change practically overnight into a wife, who will then nag, scream, sulk, and do everything she can to change him from a bad boy into a polite one, from a play-boy, say, into a provider, and so on. And he just isn't ready.

Women in general have the idea that marriage is good for men. But a lot of men find the idea of doing what a woman says is good for them restricting and reminiscent of childhood.

A woman writes, *'If he loved me, why wouldn't he commit himself for me?'* **I reply,** *'He does not commit himself for you or for love, he commits himself to you and to marriage. Think about it. It's not the same thing. Even in love, formal commitment is not a duty; it is a personal choice. It can be undertaken for its own sake only, not for anyone or anything else . . .'*

Love is no commitment whatsoever. Make of love what we will after the fact, it arrives without design and it is under no obligation. Marriage is planned and exclusive, however, and we hope (I hope we hope) married love will last a lifetime and be the basis of a family. Marriage is a commitment apart from love and one that young women in general, with the primeval tick-tock of biology in their blood, appear to be ready for as early on as ever, and certainly earlier on than men.

In short, it could be he loves the pants off you. But ready to marry, he ain't. And it's readiness, not love, that settles a man down.

There are some uncommitted men who scorn the whole institution of marriage and see their unwillingness to commit themselves to the women they love as a matter of principle. They do not wish, in other words, to commit themselves to an ideal which they do not believe in or want. 'If you loved me, you would . . .' she says, but as the die-hard bachelor sees it, it is as if she were saying to him, 'If you really loved me, you'd change your religion . . .', or, 'If you really loved me, you'd change your politics . . .', or, 'If you really loved me, you'd support my hometown football team instead of your own . . .' It seems to him that love has nothing to do with the case.

Will he *ever* be ready? Probably. As a rule, the eternal bachelor is a man more afraid of getting old than of getting married. And by far the majority of men come to terms with fidelity, habits and babies — with commitment, in other words — sooner rather than later. But not always soon enough for the girls who love them.

There are a lot of dangers in hanging around too long with a man who isn't ready for commitment: you can live on his uncommitted terms as years, even decades, slip by while you keep hoping. You can live with him through sickness and health, poverty and wealth while you keep hoping. You can have babies together and raise them to maturity, and all the while keep hoping he'll marry you.

Or it sometimes happens that after a few years he finds himself finally ready for commitment, only it's with a kid from the office he's been seeing on the sly.

Of course, there is common-law marriage and there are other contracts too, equally binding. 'Confused's' lover, for example, could imagine that signing a mortgage together for a joint piece of property is as great a commitment as marriage (and, incidentally, come the crunch as hard to get out of). But I've never heard of anyone celebrating the anniversary of the day they signed a joint mortgage, have you? 'Confused' could understandably prefer something more traditional and romantic to bind her to her lover than a shared debt to the bank. For all our fashionable talk of 'partners' and 'relationships', the longing for romance, sometimes repudiated and shameful as it is, burns just as strong in the young female heart as ever it did. Box-office hits and best-selling books bear me out.

A woman writes, *'We've been together for seven years and we have two beautiful children. But whenever I ask him to commit himself, he stalls or gets angry . . .'*
I reply, *'Seven years and a couple of kids sure sounds like a commitment to me. If, however, you want him to marry you, that's another issue . . .'*

Lots of men are scared witless of marriage because they have been married miserably in the past, or they have grown up in bad examples of the institution. Of course, just as many women have had equally awful experiences of marriage but women do not appear so easily to lose their faith in love's power to heal and restore, or so it seems from the letters I read.

Unlike most material aimed at girls, even in this day and age, the 'happy ever after' of boys' bedtime reading does not begin under a canopy or at the altar or in front of a charming old Justice of the Peace. Not for all men, to be sure, but for more of them than us, something seems to *end* with the wedding march: something marches out of the church — his freedom, his singularity, his chance of sailing off to discover a new continent or planet, his dreams, his adventures, his youth.

To be honest (what else?) I have always thought men have a point here. One of the reasons I have not been deeply tempted to affairs with married men is that I find husbands less dashing and attractive than single men of any age. Perhaps that is also one of the reasons I never wanted to marry even when I was in love: why make a husband out of a free-spirited lad?

A woman writes, *'I'm nineteen and I know I've found the man I want to spend the rest of my life with. My boyfriend is twenty. He says he loves me, but he says he's not ready to commit himself. Why is he so immature?'*
I reply, *'He's not immature for his age. He's twenty and smart. You're nineteen and immature.'*

How does a woman make a reluctant man marry her? I'm not sure I am the right agony aunt to ask. About marriage my feelings tend to be mannish. I guess the only way to lure him into marriage is to persuade him it would be 'more ideal' than what he already has. And what does he already have? In the case of 'Confused', he has a more or less unlicensed happy homelife. What more does he need?

A woman writes, *'I am twenty-four and have been living with a man for two years. We are deeply attached but when I mention marriage, he says he does not want to give up his bachelor life. What can I do? I don't seem to have any options.'*
I reply, *'He is enjoying his life, he has everything he wants, including you. Until, and if, he gets a yen for children or suddenly develops an urge for marital stability, he's not the one who will change the way things are. Why should he? If you want to make him want to change things, you will have to change first. Or you can always go on as you are. I'm not recommending you sit tight in a stalled car, only that you must see it is a valid option.*
So there it is:
1. Stay put.
2. Offer him a now-or-never ultimatum and mean it.
3. Leave and see what happens.
There are options, you see. And they are all yours . . .'

When a man is happy with things as they are, one way to encourage him to change his mind is to make his life hell on earth, I guess, though I find the idea repugnant. Call me sentimental, but I have never been able actually to recommend that a woman set about making the life of her loved one hell, even if there is a chance it will get her what she wants in the end — in this case, commitment. Torture can force anyone except a saint to recant and change his mind, but it has no place between two people who care about each other and for each other. Besides, we all know of cases where couples who have been together for ages quite happily get married suddenly and in no time are on the rocks. I suspect this happens mostly when one of the pair, not always the woman, has nagged so furiously that the other finally gives in and agrees to 'commit' himself (or herself) in front of witnesses. When marriage is undertaken as a last resort to save the troubled union, even if the union was troubled in the first place because one of the couple wanted marriage and the other did not, more harm can be done to the fabric of love than either lover realises at the time.

First comes marriage to help two people pull through a rough patch in a love affair, next comes a baby to help them pull through the trouble in the marriage, and finally comes divorce to put an end to their misery and alienation. (Yes, yes, I know, many cohabiting couples marry eventually and are as happy, even happier, than newly wed virgins. However, 'Confused' and her lover are in the *other* group and I am addressing myself to her problem.)

There used to be a lot of gruesome old wives' strictures against cohabitation that boiled down to lines like, 'Why should a man buy the cow if he gets the milk free?' Repellent though the notion is, I'm afraid it often holds quite true even now. Sexual pragmatism is not just for men, by the by. It also applies to all those girls who view marriage as a prize for being good (in bed, too, they hope) and who are deeply offended when they have been as good as they know how, and yet he has failed to give them the reward they believe they have earned. Close, but no cigar.

Judging from all I have observed, every exclusive union quite early on has a marrying moment: a peak time when her hopes are at their highest and (usually) his fears are at their lowest. If that unguarded, impetuous moment passes without a proposal, it can be a long wait to have it back again; it may never reoccur. Mind you, when the marrying moment does return at last to a couple who know each other well and see each other clearly, and who want each other still, what could give better odds than marriage at that point?

A woman writes, *'We've been together for eight years, since I was nineteen. He says he loves me but he doesn't want to marry me or anyone, ever. Should I stay with him. Or would I just be wasting more of my time . . .?*
I reply, *'If you really see life with him as a waste of time unless he marries*

you, then being married means more to you than he does. In other words, you are not committed to him. And that's fair enough. But what choice have you got? Get out.'

When one lover wants commitment (marriage) and the other hates the whole idea, they have arrived at a perfect stalemate.

She: 'If he loved me, he'd marry me . . .'
He: 'If she loved me, she wouldn't ask me to go against my dislike of the whole idea . . .'

What does a player do in a stalemate situation? She outwaits her opponent, pitting her nerve against his. Or she backs away to play another game. Or she cheats when his back is turned.

For lessons in how to cheat a man into marriage, if that's what 'Confused' chooses to do, I am a little too fastidious to consult. But there are doubtless back-street agony aunts who could help her. Or there is always her mother and her putative mother-in-law to add their muscle and turn the screws.

As far as I can see it, any woman in a long-term love affair who knows she will never be happy without a conventional marriage, if the man is not amenable, has to decide for herself which matters more to her: living with him and risking being forever 'Miss', or leaving him to fulfil herself as another man's 'Mrs'? Her decision will depend upon how important marriage is to her as an ideal, and how much she needs the security of tradition and a conventional shelter in which to raise children.

Leaving, like staying — like any decision — will be effective only when undertaken positively (even if sorrowfully). She has to leave in order to search for the security which she knows she needs more in the long run than she needs to be with this particular man. Of course, it could be that he will come to his senses, follow her, fall on one knee, and offer up the traditional diamond. But getting what she wants when she gambles is in the luck of the draw, and it is not something anyone can ever count on.

So far my thinking about the problem of commitment has been one-sided. But I think I sniff a growing trend among young women as well as young men to be increasingly hesitant about committing themselves. Or am I myself a victim of wishful thinking? I do wish girls would make more original and adventurous use of their youth.

Admittedly, when an editor asked me not long ago to write a piece about young women who were in no hurry for commitment, examples were not thick on the ground. And those I came up with were all urban, ambitious, career women, many of whom, I fear, will be writing to an agony aunt in ten years' time saying they feel unfulfilled, and asking where they can find Mr Wonderful.

Young people complain when old crumplies like me hark back to bygone times. They prefer to think they have arrived in the present with no strings attached, while at the same time, I notice, they cannot wait to attach their own strings to the future. But the fact is, like it or not, we continue to be born with a greater or lesser commitment to what was done before we were so much as a gleam in daddy's eye.

Once upon a time, girl babies arrived slated for eventual marriage, probably to a man of whom their parents approved. Or they undertook conventional spinsterhood, most likely as a caretaker of the very young or the very old. Or they lived out a socially acceptable variation of the themes above. By and large, they had little if any say in the matter of their commitment. As surely, mind you, were men born to succeed to the family profession or follow in an inherited trade and to do pretty much as daddy had done, only better. Neither sex was born free from responsibility, or ever will be, but men generally have been confined in a more open prison than women.

Of course there were exceptional women who rejected their precommitted destiny and devoted themselves to art, religion, adventure, commerce or wickedness — to some area of life not ordinarily part of the female inheritance. (I cannot for the moment recall any genuine examples of men who have joyously rejected *their* more worldly birthright in favour of committing themselves utterly to hearth and nursery. Can you tell me why that should be?) Generally speaking, though, once upon a time we were pretty much *born* committed to one way of life over all others.

At last, after untold struggle, we women have been freed, if imperfectly, into the opportunity to commit ourselves to, amongst other things, a home and a family. And why not, if that is what we choose? But also and as well to commit ourselves in as many other ways as we have gifts and energy.

Granted, it is still more difficult for a woman to succeed on the wider stages of commerce, politics, the arts or business. But it is a damn sight easier now than ever before. There are people working to make it easier still. And nature has given us the equipment for the extraordinary triumph of motherhood if we wish it. The world is not a half-bad place for a woman nowadays. I for one would not choose to come back as a human male, not until they redesigned the critter, tucked his sex in a safer location, and scaled down his ego to match his capabilities.

Commitment is still destiny, yes, but it is no longer pinned to us in the cradle. Nevertheless, nine out of ten young women when they use the word 'commitment', at least in the hearing of an agony aunt, refer only to the age-old concept: they still expect not just that their sole serious commitment in life will be to a man but, even more, they want a corresponding commitment in return. Now, I can see the point of marriage being one commitment among several, but I will never see how it can be the first or even the main commitment in an interesting and creative life, whether his or hers.

A woman writes, *'This summer I've been given the chance to travel abroad alone for three to four months. I am twenty-one and have been with my boyfriend for three years. We are happy and want to get married. However, I'm torn between wanting to be with him and taking this wonderful opportunity. He says there is a possibility that we'll split up if I go. How can I decide? I want to have my cake and eat it, which I know isn't possible . . .'*

I reply, *'Do you know what happens to cake if you don't eat it? It turns green and mouldy and dries out and has to be thrown away. Life's a cake! Enjoy it. How in the world does this man expect a lifelong union with you if he cannot wait even a few short months without threatening a split? At your age, if your ambitions are not compatible with the man you love and are not supported by him, then my advice must be to scrap the man. There is more than one man for one woman out there, but unsatisfied ambitions never have a second chance.'*

A second woman writes, *'A year ago I got engaged to my loving and supportive boyfriend of two years. I am twenty, in my last year of college, and he is twenty-eight. When I graduate I want to travel and work abroad, but I also want to be with him. He can't wait until I get a job so we can buy a house, and I want this eventually too. But not now . . .'*

I reply, *'The youth of a liberated woman seems to me better spent in discovery of the world and herself than in service to future security or early commitment. Love and practically everything come more than once in a lifetime. But youth? Honey, this is it . . .'*

An ideal marriage remains the ideal way to raise children, and children *are* a commitment: we cannot return them to the sender or exchange them for a better fit. Women who want children have to adjust their ambitions and their calendars to suit, and for most of us that will always mean marriage. But not a hasty one, I hope, not one undertaken automatically as the *only* imaginable commitment, and never as an excuse to neglect other commitments which we all inherit or the duties that women have been liberated to share: commitment to friendship, to work, to understanding, duties to ourselves, and to the community of which we are a part.

● ● ● ● ● ● ● ● ● ●

Dear 'Confused',

He engaged himself to you three years ago. Now he has decided he doesn't want to marry. Anyone. Ever. And he says not to take it personally! How does he expect you to take it, I wonder? It concerns a pretty personal part of your life, and I hope you've told him that. I am not saying I think he should marry you. You've been with him since you were very, very young — you're still very, very young — and I wonder if you aren't a little too keen right now on marrying him?

You say you're in a muddle. And at the same time you tell me you feel let down and cheated, and you are not prepared to stick around without commitment. That doesn't sound very muddled to me. He has no intention of committing himself, you have no intention of sticking around without commitment. Where's the muddle? Don't confuse being confused with being reluctant. You're not confused. It is just that you are understandably not very eager to leave him, and it is going to be difficult. But haven't you as good as told me you are going to have to get out and seek commitment somewhere else? What else can you do? I have no magic wand to wave at him and make him change his mind. (And if I had a magic wand, I'd be very, very slow ever to use it.)

How does a woman get commitment? Commitment is not something anyone can demand from another person. Commitment, it seems to me, is something we seek all our lives to give, not to get. When you, and you alone, are committed to what you want, heart and mind and soul, the rest falls into place.

Yours,

Aunt Irma

• • • • • • • • • •

AGONY AUNT'S WORKSHEET

1. Name six ways a lover shows commitment, starting with the *least* important.
2. Do we have any choice about our own commitments?
3. If 'Confused' were committed to her lover, would she care whether or not he married her?
4. Can there be love without commitment?
5. Can there be commitment without love?
6. How far do you think 'Confused', or any woman, can go to make a reluctant lover marry her without laying down resentment and trouble for the future?
7. Would you call time in love wasted if your lover failed to commit himself?
8. If love doesn't last a lifetime, is it love?
9. Write your own reply to 'Confused'.

PROBLEM THREE

Sex is fun — what's an orgasm?

• • • • • • • • • •

Dear Irma,

I don't think I've ever had an orgasm. I've always enjoyed sex, so it hasn't really bothered me before. But now I'm with a guy I really care for, and he is starting to get upset. He says all his other girlfriends always had orgasms, and it makes him feel inadequate when I don't. Please help.

'Non-O'

• • • • • • • • • •

If Queen Victoria ever had orgasms, she kept mum about it; Freud didn't see any real need for women to have them; lots of feminists, early and late, thought orgasm (of the vaginal variety, at least) was a myth put about by men, presumably to make us worry about ourselves. It's only within living memory that women have been generally supposed to have orgasms. Before that, we had beaux, lovers, husbands; we had babies, we had headaches, sometimes we had a good time; but orgasms? Not so you'd talk about them, thank you.

Then, in the seventies, about the same time I started writing the Agony column, it seemed every third letter dealt with orgasms and two out of three of those were complaints from women who had never had one. 'Frigid', used formerly to describe a female incapable of arousal, became overnight a victim to early political correctness; sensitive people replaced it with a solemn 'non-orgasmic', or the perfectly disgusting 'sexually dysfunctional'.

Sexual problems continued to pour into the Agony column, of course, but as we moved along far fewer letters were specifically concerned with an inability to achieve climax, and now it is only about two in ten. Whether or not complaints have decreased because of an increase in orgasmic women over recent years, I cannot say for sure. My guess is that the very great emphasis on sex in the media, and the widespread advertising of the clitoris and G-spot, particularly in the materialistic eighties, managed to blow away a lot of the ignorance and inhibitions that prevented women of other generations from having orgasms, or even admitting they knew what orgasms were.

In the main, that is a very good thing, but any agony aunt who has not gone soft in the head must remind you that in a world as rich in choices as ours, and which is growing ever richer for women, everything we take means rejecting other things: for every gain we make, we suffer losses — that's why decision-making is such an agonising business for us. Furthermore, there is no way out of making decisions: *not* deciding is deciding, too.

Back in the bad old days I sometimes advised women who were going crazy trying to have orgasms to have something else instead: a rollicking good time in bed, for instance, fun in the bath, passion, affection, comfort and fidelity. Now that more women seem to be able to climax all over the place, or so they tell me, I find myself advising them to be sure while they're at it to remember to hang on to all those other good things too.

No sooner did men find their way to the clitoris, develop staying power and start to catch on at last to female orgasms than womankind at large seemed to decide to get real. Reality is as usual a mixed bag: the reality is, some women have orgasms every time, many women have orgasms most of the time, most women have orgasms some of the time, and some women never have orgasms at all — a few of *them* not because they can't, but because they do not know how.

Those who do not know how to have orgasms have never masturbated, I guess. Or if they have, it must have been with a singular lack of enthusiasm. Women have written to me who obviously confuse approaching orgasm with an urge to urinate, and so stop themselves short of the top (to spare the sheets, I imagine, though clean sheets have never been a gauge of good sex).

'What is sex like?' I asked an older more experienced girl when I was about ten. 'Very sticky,' she replied. And as far as it went, it turned out to be an accurate and vivid description.

A woman writes, *'I am twenty . . . I masturbate . . . not every day, but it makes me feel dirty and unclean. Whenever I do, something bad happens . . . I get into bad debt, I fight with my boyfriend or my mum. I try to stop but in two or three months, I do it again . . . I feel guilty and ashamed and the bad luck starts. How can I kick the habit?'*
I reply, *'There is nothing intrinsically wrong with masturbation: it does not harm anyone, it does not cheat anyone, it does not cause acne, madness, blindness, baldness or "runs of bad luck" . . . not unless you decide to punish yourself for your pleasure.'*

Masturbation is one way for anyone to measure the sensation of orgasm and learn the best way to arrive at it. Then, she can tell her lover how to get her to a climax — if she is bold enough. I used to recommend talking frankly in bed, but I now think that talking dirty in bed is probably more effective and certainly more sexy than talking frankly. And anyhow, I suspect not many young women are bold enough, or unromantic enough about sex, or ever have been, to put their preference to a lover in so many words. An easier plan, and much more fun, is to steer him in the right direction with sounds of pleasure, then, when he's getting it right, with that classic phrase of basic sexual technique: 'Don't stop.'

I wonder if 'Non-O' masturbates? In the seventies and eighties, defence of masturbation was such an important part of an agony aunt's job, my accountant was only half-joking when he suggested I ask vibrator manufacturers for a commission. I'm surprised self-pleasuring still needs to be advocated in this enlightened day and age, but 'Non-O' must have slipped through the net. Orgasms vary in intensity at different times in everyone's life and there is no reason to assume that their strength does not also vary from person to person. However, I cannot help but think that if 'Non-O' *had* masturbated she would know for sure whether or not she'd reached orgasm instead of saying she doesn't *think* she has.

In the past, letter-writers on this topic used to say, 'I've never had an orgasm and it makes me feel disappointed and inadequate . . .' Recently, they are a lot more likely to say, 'I don't have orgasms, and it makes *him* feel disappointed and inadequate.' Is that progress or is that progress? Yes, I guess it probably *is* progress. Because in the old days, no sooner did women find out they were expected to have orgasms than they began to fake them. Now, why on earth does a woman fake an orgasm? To make him 'feel good about himself', why else?

God only knows how many women have routinely faked orgasms, honest women too, women who would not dream of lying to their lovers on any other score, women who would swear under oath that they believed truth and mutual trust to be the linchpins of a solid union. And why go to such lengths to make a man 'feel good about himself', even at the sacrifice of dignity and truth? Because you fear that, now perhaps more than ever, he will leave you if you don't, and find someone else who does — 'Oooooh, aaaah, you're the greatest!' — even if she is lying through her teeth.

The point is not whether faking is a 'good' or 'bad' thing for women to do, you know. If men could fake orgasms as easily as women, no doubt they would do it too sometimes to wind things down to a reasonable conclusion, particularly when they have a meeting in the morning, say, and the alarm clock is set to go off at six a.m. (A man I know has finally persuaded me, incidentally, that men *can* fake it too, to a greater degree than most women imagine, though he concedes that they are nowhere near as brilliant at faking it as us.)

But the big trouble with lies in general is that they box the liar into a corner where the truth becomes lonely and hard and increasingly difficult *ever* to reveal. Once a woman starts faking orgasm as a matter of course, if she then decides she wants the real thing, having gone to operatic lengths to persuade her man he is an infallible top gun, how does she stop lying to him?

At least 'Non-O' is upfront about her motive for wanting an orgasm, even if that motive is as timorous and modest as ever: to make *him* happy.

A woman writes, *'My boyfriend and I have tried all sorts of positions and games. Sometimes I "come" during foreplay but I have never been able to orgasm with him inside me. He doesn't know and I don't want him to worry about it, because I love him very much and our lovemaking is wonderful for me, even when I don't have an orgasm. Do I have a problem?'*

I reply, *'You must have a problem. Only people with problems write to agony aunts . . .'*

A lot of girls who complain about a failure to have regular orgasms say they really truly adore sex and find it thrilling, even though they rarely climax, and hardly ever during penetration. Men would find it hard to believe, I think, how many women *can* enjoy sexual fulfilment without obligatory orgasms. I found it hard to believe too in my pioneering days, but I've started to wonder now whether we have been so smart after all to isolate orgasm from the erotic whole and put it at the level of a punchline, without which there is no story.

A clinical element has crept into our sexual encounters, replacing love and lovers with concepts more suitable for the boardroom than the bedroom. It's almost as if we are somehow trying to turn lovemaking into an activity less feminine, more aggressive and mannish and goal-bound; as if making love were not one of the few remaining activities of life where warmth, softness and tenderness can outweigh, outclass and outmanoeuvre the harsh and competitive values that are running the rest of the world.

For good and for ill, the biggest difference between the sexes is sex. Men have a tendency by nature, encouraged by nurture, to be goal-orientated in a way that women have not yet quite achieved and, in spite of a few well-publicised football-playing girls, probably never will. (Anyhow, I hope we don't: the devoted pursuit of a ball towards a net or hole of any kind is a frivolous waste of passion. I have faith that women are too smart and too well-occupied ever to see scoring points as anything more than an amusement.)

A woman writes, *'Dear Irma, I have multiple orgasms almost every time my boyfriend and I make love. Seven was my highest. This is not the sort of topic to bring up at a dinner party, so I do not know for sure if it is exceptional . . .'*

I reply, *'Come again? I don't quite catch what's bothering you . . .?'*

As a general rule, arousal has not got the hair-trigger for women it has for men: excitement is not so localised, nor is its aim so basic. Whether or not we have babies is a matter of personal choice, whether or not we want them is up to each of us, but free will and choice cannot alter our anatomy — nor who can say how much of our instinctive and psychic energy. We have been designed and programmed by Mother Nature to conceive and carry a foetus to term. She's a great mother, is nature, but she's sure as hell no sister.

Like it or not, lovemaking always has the potential of a big production number for a girl.

Even though the classic wham-bam is part of the established sexual repertoire, only anal intercourse is less popular than the habitual 'quickie', which, going by the vast number of letters I have received on the topic, never holds pride of place with women. Orgasm is the highest point along the way of making love, but women who write to me say they revel just as much in all that happens before, and a lot of them complain of the absence of any caresses afterwards.

Ironically, one of the best methods by which a woman can achieve her elusive orgasm is consciously *not* to chase it next time she makes love, but to ask her lover to spend a night, or a weekend, being erotic without penetration. Sex is playful. Sex is fun. Sex is sexy. But when everything in you is screaming 'Will I? Won't I?', sex is a chore and plain boring.

Tender, patient and attentive touching, massaging, caressing — to say nothing of heavier fun involving fantasies, role-playing and sex toys — by making orgasm a much smaller element of a much greater whole, are much more likely to serve it up to a woman who has never had one before, or who has a lot of trouble on that score.

Of course, no man can be *that* tender, patient and attentive every time, nor every woman always be in the mood for it. But it isn't a bad idea to schedule on a pretty regular basis long, slow sessions of love-making without any need for either partner to do anything more than wallow in erotic pleasure. A friend of mine says she and her lover call these their 'parties we both attend, but nobody has to come'.

Because of the nature of female arousal and because she is generally less afraid of sensuality (which a lot of men find a 'feminine' concept — alien, and rather spooky too, at least until they get the hang of it), the woman is very often the one who must initiate the more sensual aspects of lovemaking.

'You women can just lie there,' a man once told me bitterly, 'but a guy has to get it up or nothing happens.' Could that be why nature made men goal- and prey-orientated? Because otherwise, they would be as slow to become sexually aroused as many women are? Given the leonine lazy sods a lot of men are, if arousal were any trouble to achieve, they might not even be bothered to try.

As things stand (or not), problems in the sex department scream 'failure' at a man, and for the very reason that men tend to keep an eye on the target and are, in the main, competitive by training and nature, failure hits them hard, especially if they are failing at something all their chums and workmates are boasting about having done perfectly the night before.

'Dear Irma, We used to make love all the time. Now I'm lucky if it's once a month. When I complain about it, he says he's satisfied, and what's my problem?'

For every complaint I receive from a woman who has trouble reaching orgasm, two arrive from women whose lovers get there too fast, and three more from those whose men have practically stopped trying. It's a bother, isn't it, that ego is the primary male sex organ? It means every sexual encounter for a man is to some degree a challenge, and thus any problem or shade of criticism whatsoever threatens a stunning blow first to his ego, thereafter to his erection. That's why it is so very hard to make your average man bravely face up to the simple fact that the phrase 'What's your problem?' has no significance at all between lovers: if one partner in sex has a problem with what is going on, then so does the other one.

When a man is a lousy lover, or hardly a lover at all, a woman's first job, before they can work on the condition or go for counselling, is to persuade him there really is room for improvement. Making a man sit still and discuss sexual problems he does not realise or want to admit exist is a very, very tough job. Whining, shouting or screaming will probably force him to retreat into silence, or down to the bar. Men by and large hate a scene. Bullying and threats of infidelity have no place between two people with feelings for each other. As for casting blame, it hurts and puts him on the defensive, and in the end is no more helpful than casting stones.

Don't ever fool yourself that because he is a man he lacks all feelings; he does feel pain too, believe me, only because he hates it as a weakness in himself, he is generally much less able to express it except as anger.

Tact, gentleness and seduction are the most courteous and effective ways to approach your mate on issues of sex, just as you would have him approach you if the shoe were on the other foot (as it sometimes is). Do not go into a serious discussion of sexual incompatibility without being prepared, all arguments marshalled, and the number of a counsellor ready to ring if he agrees to see one with you. Of all areas of contention between couples, the sexual one responds most easily, even pleasantly, to counselling once the recalcitrant partner has been persuaded to try. If all else fails and he refuses to change his style or seek advice, or if he will not be seduced into making love as often as you'd like, you have to decide for yourself what you need from the relationship, and how far you are willing to go to get it.

Separation is not always a bad idea, nor need it be permanent; leaving him certainly shows you mean business. Time and space apart from each other lets things fall into perspective and gives both people a chance to cool down and decide whether they can reinstate themselves as lovers, or friends, or neither. Bear in mind, however, that a couple apart can come to opposing decisions. He might go off with someone else, too. So might she. Temporary separation always carries the risk of becoming for keeps. Separations sometimes help resolve big problems such as facing up to sexual incompatibility, but they are a gamble: the only people who can afford to gamble are those who can afford to lose.

When a woman lacks all self-sufficiency and is terrified above all of losing her man, such as he is, then the stakes are too high for her to chance a trial separation. She will have to find another way — as persuasive as leaving but less risky — to make him aware of how serious their problem is. I cannot imagine what that could be. A vengeful infidelity, perhaps? To get even with him for his insensitivity. Cowardly, and not a good idea. Nagging? Tears? Long silences? As hard on her as they are on him, and also habit-forming but not always effective. Or will she, if she has developed no resources for independence and does not dare even risk losing him, simply have to knuckle under and surrender to the way things are?

There really are harder things to achieve in this life than an orgasm and, to be quite honest, there are more important things, too. I guess that is easy for me to say, not so easy for a woman who wants to have one but can't, to understand or accept. Nevertheless, I do hope 'Non-O' manages to feel the genuine rush and astonishment of a climax, and I don't know any reason why she shouldn't. After that, if she decides to fake it from time to time, at least she will know how to turn in an Academy Award-winning performance.

• • • • • • • • • •

Dear 'Non-O',

Orgasms are delirious fun: what you are after is fun, in other words, not purpose, or true love, or the holy grail. Don't chase an orgasm, let it catch you. First off, however, you'd better make sure you know what it is. Orgasm is also called 'climax' because that describes it precisely: the release of sexual excitement when for a few moments mind and body explode like fireworks. If you see lovemaking as a series of peaks, orgasm is the one that goes off the scale. Once an orgasm is under way, it is out of control which, I believe, is the very reason some women are afraid of it.

I'm sure you've felt excitement, all alone, from accidental or deliberate self-stimulation. You would be wise to set out deliberately to masturbate beyond the point where previously you stopped. If you are uninhibited enough, your boyfriend could give you a hand, as it were. Otherwise, do it alone, let your thoughts loose, and continue right the way to climax. You will know it when it happens because nothing much more can happen. Some women have multiple orgasms. But I have been a believer all my life in quality, not quantity; I do not envy them, and once you have found your way to your own climax, there is no reason to envy anyone.

As soon as you're sure you know exactly the sensation you are after, you and your boyfriend can go in pursuit of it as often as you both wish. Slowly, slowly wins this race, remember. As a matter of fact, why don't you put aside one night to make endless love, having decided beforehand not to let an orgasm stop you or come between you. That will show you what levels of excitement you can achieve while relieving you of the need to take orgasm so

57

damned seriously that it pre-empts love, closeness, delight, and pleasure in each other's bodies.

And while we're talking pleasure, oral sex (by him) is a well-travelled and practically irresistible route to orgasm. I wonder if either of you has an insurmountable prejudice against it? If so, a scented bath (together?) could ease inhibitions and a bedside jar of honey, though it adds calories and is hell on the sheets, has been known to work a treat.

> *Cheerfully,*
> *Aunt Irma*

● ● ● ● ● ● ● ● ● ●

AGONY AUNT'S WORKSHEET

1. Name six things sex is *for*.
2. Can you imagine a man and woman in love who do not make love? Under what circumstances?
3. If a woman does not have an orgasm, do you think:
    a. She has failed
    b. He has failed
    c. Love has failed
    d. Nothing and nobody have failed?
4. Is faking an orgasm the same as lying? Why or why not?
5. What are the qualities of a great lover's technique, starting with the *least* important?
6. Think of three things 'Non-O' might do to make her lover sexier.
7. Write your own answer to her letter.

PROBLEM FOUR

Can there be love without trouble?

• • • • • • • • • •

Dear Irma,

My boyfriend and I have been living together for nearly two years and we knew each other for a year before that. I'm twenty-two, he's twenty-eight. In the beginning our sex life was great and then it tapered off. Recently we hardly make love more than once a week if I'm lucky, and it's all over in minutes. He's just started his own business and I know he's worried about it, so I try not to push it. But the other day when I was looking through his desk I found a girlie magazine. Also, I found a porn video in his old suitcase at the back of a closet. The thought of him looking at that stuff makes me sick. Why can't I be all he needs? Please help me. I'm so unhappy.

'In Pain'

• • • • • • • • • •

Pornography is found under the beds of rapists and mass murderers. But if you were to look, you'd also find it under the beds of lawyers, judges, policemen and other pillars of society.

'Do you see all those well-dressed men?' a university professor of sociology asked me (we were flying together to a seminar, and the airport was awash with business-class travellers). 'There's a girlie magazine in every briefcase. Bet on it,' he said. For every woman who poses in a dirty magazine or wiggles around in a porno video, there are hundreds, even thousands of men who will get off just looking at her. If porn demeans anyone, and I am not persuaded it does, then statistically it demeans mostly men.

I find it thought-provoking, incidentally, that far and away the majority of women who write to the Agony column about their lovers' porn complain not that it demeans us all by presenting us as sex objects, but rather, like 'In Pain', they are hurt because the celluloid charmers in porn make them feel that they are not sex objects *enough*.

A man I know calls his susceptibility to the visual image 'the flash mechanism'; he maintains it is as ancient a response in malekind as the racing heartbeat of a hunter when his prey leaps into sight. In my friend's experience, which is immense, men respond sexually to pictures, and women to the more wistful allure of words. Any heterosexual male free from trauma or inhibition enjoys looking at an attractive female body, whether or not it is the one he's pledged to love and honour. When he's down, it lifts his spirits; when he's fretful, it soothes him; and when he is in danger it reminds him that bodies were not given to us merely so we could dispatch them to kingdom come. Soldiers in a war zone don't care any less for their girlfriends and wives at home just because there are nudie pinups spreadeagled over their bunks. A picture of a naked woman makes her an object, that is true enough, but no more so than a photo of a doctor's wife framed in silver on his desk.

Porn is accused of instigating violence against women, but in fact far and away the majority of pornographic plots and films are not concerned with coercion but with sex-mad cuties who get off even faster than the guy, and who require nothing from him — no special caresses, no foreplay, no affection, no reassurances, no commitment, no money, no tender concern — nothing except more, more, more.

In practically all other areas of life there are countless discrepancies between the sexes, but in most pornography there is equality, of desire and of power. For every young man who jerks off over an air-brushed image, there is a girl building erotic fantasies around the sugary goo of a paperback bodice-ripper. Is there really so much difference between the two? Only that the man forgets his dreamboat the moment he's finished and walks away from the whole incident a lot faster than the girl, who never altogether abandons her romantic daydreams, least of all when she's in the arms of a flesh-and-blood lover.

'In Pain's' letter made me think about the time around a million years ago when I was down and out in London and found a job at last with a small publicity agency. Our main (only!) client decided one Monday morning to stop being merely the proprietor of a few clubs, and to turn himself into the Hugh Hefner of Great Britain. Thus, by Tuesday I found myself on an editorial board, set to produce the first English-language girlie magazine outside the United States. Not my proudest moment, perhaps, but a whole lot better than going on the streets.

Our biggest problem, by the by, was not to find women ready to strip for the camera, but to stop those who really shouldn't. Droves of them applied in answer to an advertisement we placed in a national paper; we looked at photographs of naked housewives, naked secretaries, naked bank clerks, as well as a lot of professional models and strippers, taut and depilated as marble. Me, I always liked bones, strong lines, and faces ready to spit in a man's eye at twenty paces, but in a short time I started to recognise the quality of unquestioning acquiescence that my male bosses were looking for in their stroke-maidens. 'These aren't supposed to be *real* women,' one of the senior editors tried to explain to me. 'They're like sexual icons.'

When it comes to their sexual icons, love does not signify. Men in search of fantasy thrills mostly want a tootsie who advertises availability, no strings and, with a few dominatrices thrown in for spice, they go mainly for a semblance of eager, uncritical complicity: a face and posture that says to a man whatever he wants, she wants it just as much — the sort of female a man could get the hots for, fuck, satisfy, then leave happy and guiltlessly just by turning the page.

A woman writes, *'Dear Irma, my boyfriend and I have been together for* *nearly three years. Recently I found out that he had bought ten pornographic magazines off my brother. They had agreed not to tell me. My boyfriend told me it was just a stage guys go through, but we are both very sexually active. Ever since I found out, I've been miserable. I cry my eyes out, feeling so stupid, like I didn't please him. How could my own brother do that to me?'* **I reply,** *'He did not think it mattered. To be honest, neither do I. But as it matters to you, it's something you'll have to talk to your boyfriend about and thrash out together, until you are both happy with the solution . . .'*

When I fail to attack pornography wholesale, and choose instead to reply honestly to letters like this, I get a very angry response from readers. But I am glad to say I am not a politician; I am not looking for 'In Pain's' vote. I do not need to worry about disagreement or toe a party line; I have no incentive to lie about what I genuinely hold to be true. And I genuinely hold it to be true that pornography in general does our society infinitely less harm than crackpot cults, psuedo-therapies, racist doctrine, Barbie-doll role models for little girls, confessional television programmes aimed mostly at female viewers (primetime agony hours, I mean, hosted by a new breed of celebrity, which glamorise victimisation, trivialise our common responsibilities and insidiously encourage competitive moaning), Hollywood standards of hope, soap-opera ethics, and a whole lot more schlock that we tolerate easily and even defend.

It is no more difficult to sympathise with a man's recourse to sure-fire pornography (especially if he is having stress in his life) than to understand a woman's occasional out-of-bounds trip to the refrigerator for a solitary 'go' at the chocolate ice-cream. Most men outgrow pornography, in any case, as their sex urges become mature. Pornography has been with us since the Romans and before, but recently it has become a political issue, and that means we have to race to a 'pro' or 'anti' position, sign petitions and cease to discuss the subject calmly or treat it with an open mind. Seesaw polemics of this nature do not advance anything but trouble. By forcing us to choose sides, they put a moratorium on weighing the evidence; by presenting topics as 'good' or 'bad', they turn discussion into personal abuse, and prevent us from acknowledging matters of degree.

There is porn, in other words, and there is porn. When it involves those who have been recruited too young to know what they are doing, or when it is sold in places where it is inappropriate and offensive, then naturally the community at large has a right to object, as they do to the sale of alcohol. Pornographic magazines are made for masturbation. They are as functional as cookbooks, and a man always has the ingredients to hand. Most men think of masturbation as a sex act altogether apart from love and no more like making love than watering a lawn is like, say, surfing. The moving image on the screen, a voice talking dirty, a photograph, are kick-starters for erection and release which, while they are going on, relieve the man of all other concerns. What's more, a man need not fear failure to maintain an erection, or failure to satisfy anyone except himself.

'Porn is so uncomplicated,' said a chum I consult on such issues. 'And life is hard. I'm crazy about my girlfriend. But sometimes I want to indulge my sex drive, without a thought to love, or caring, or someone else's enjoyment. Why not?'

Cries from the heart like that of 'In Pain' arrive so often on my desk they must indicate a confusion in women between *anything* the slightest bit sexy and love itself. Yet it is my impression that Misses April, May, June and July are interchangeable as far as men are concerned and their porn princesses are a lot less real to them than, say, movie stars are to a whole lot of women. Letters arrive quite regularly from young and not so young *Cosmo* readers confessing devotion to pop stars and movie stars, and sometimes even asking seriously how they can find their idol's address, because they know, just know, they are meant for each other.

A woman writes, *'Dear Irma, I'm horribly worried that I am being unfaithful to my boyfriend because I think of Keanu Reeves whenever he touches me . . .'*

I reply, *'You are no more being unfaithful to your boyfriend than you are being unfaithful to Keanu Reeves . . .'*

Admittedly, the movie-star phenomenon is not yet as widespread, at least among adult females, as porn is among males, especially young ones. But the reckless way we women confuse carnal desire with love when it comes to star adulation is so widespread as to have caught my interest, and I am waiting to see a paper on it by some bright-eyed psychology major. All in all, it is a more solitary fantasy mode than porn — not many men would be all that pleased to inhabit an image of Keanu Reeves while they are caressing their girlfriends. On the other hand, plenty of women find some varieties of pornography titillating too, and it can be shared. Why not? Couples have found that watching it together, even shopping for it, adds zip to a flagging sex life.

Fertility clinics could hardly guarantee a constant supply of fresh semen without pornography. Nobody will ever know how many youngsters now and to come will have Misses April, May and June to thank for their very existence.

Having put forward a mild enough defence of porn in response to 'In Pain's' letter, the time has come to balance the books. A problem exists when a lover's masturbation replaces sexual contact with the real woman in his union. Also, discourtesy is repellent, and when two people are in love and live together, it is the utmost discourtesy for one of them to use or display in their common space *any* material which gives genuine offence to the other. Thus, if neither her boy-friend nor I can persuade 'In Pain' that his girlie magazines are really quite innocuous, then the ardour of a lover and common courtesy, alas not common enough, require him to scrap them.

By the same token, however, flatmates and lovers alike need areas of privacy, even if it is no more than a desk drawer or 'an old suitcase at the back of the closet' where the other never intrudes. 'She who peeks through keyholes,' my old mother says, 'never sees anything very nice.'

A woman writes, *'Dear Irma, one day last month I came home early from work and found my boyfriend in our bedroom dressed up in my clothes. He said he was curious about how it felt, but I think there is more to it than that. We've always had a good sex life. Why is he doing this to me? Is he gay?'*

Troubled and hurt though 'In Pain' is by her boyfriend's stash of porn, there are women who write to me in perplexity far, far greater, including those who discover, sometimes after many years, that the man they live with has a deep sexual secret. Quite often he is a trans-vestite, or cross-dresser. It is not something he is doing 'to her', it is something he is driven to do by deep urges of his own which he may be ashamed and frightened to share with her, or indeed anyone. All I can do for women who write about cross-dressing lovers is, first of all, mitigate the shock or disgust they may feel at their dis-covery by assuring them that cross-dressing is a separate issue from homosexuality.

Transvestites are not always gay. Maybe their preference for women's clothes derives from an early sensual encounter with silks.

Maybe its source is something quite mundane. Certainly the trans-vestites I have known were of a domestic turn and had a very old-fashioned dress sense. Whatever the cause, a transvestite's sexual thrill is attached to the sensation of being done up in our gear, just as a lot of us women, too, get a sexy feeling from the makeup and clothes we wear, and wear certain clothes when we want to feel sexy. I've had two or three men friends over the years who turned out, incidentally, to be transvestites, and I have seen them in their glad rags, but I cannot say for sure that I could happily make love with a cross-dresser. Who knows? My ability to do so has never been tested. I hear tell that sometimes women learn to enjoy helping their lovers choose makeup and clothes. True enough, though, some letters along these lines land on my desk with the unmistakable 'thunk' of phoneys, written by men to excite themselves, or simply prompted by their own wishful thinking. Phoney letters in general go into too much salacious physical detail — they never leave bad enough alone:

(S)he writes, *'Irma, the woman next door insists on dressing her little boy like a girl. Yesterday he was wearing a little red pinafore with white daisies on the pockets and little patent leather shoes with white socks . . . whenever he's naughty, she even forces him to wear a long blond wig, poor tyke. Should I get in touch with the authorities . . .?'*
I reply, *'Write again and include your address, and I'd be glad to put the authorities in touch with you . . .'*

From time to time a letter arrives from a writer who gets a kick out of dressing up her partner and then taking him out to shop or to a restaurant, which must be risky ventures: the transvestites I know are pretty hunky. Sometimes, even when such letters are clearly genuinely being written by the girlfriend, it's my impression that the guy is looking over her shoulder in gleeful humiliation. I have a hunch that when a stronger sexual orientation does attach to cross-dressing, it is not homosexuality so much as male masochism and a taste for bondage. I have always found high heels perfect agony to wear so I *would* think that, I guess.

For a lot of women it is hardly any trouble at all to introduce some girlie magazines and porn into the scheme of things without a trace of 'In Pain's' distress. If he were my man, I know I'd rather he had his wicked way and turned the page or fast-forwarded than made it a habit to bed my friends or have sex with acquiescent whores, especially without benefit of condom.

I am not saying a man *has* to do beastly things, by the by, or that men have a more brute nature than ours which they are driven to indulge and which we ought to tolerate. I am merely saying that fantasies are on a different level from deeds involving other human beings, and I hold to the general male view that masturbation, if it does not affect a man's primary sexual relationship, is nobody's business but his own. As for the partners of transvestites, mercifully they have a great support system which I feel happy to recommend.

To say every woman *should* cheerfully accept her lover's cross-dressing would be as cruel and pointless as to say she *should* accept his pornography. But love *can* assuredly stretch to incredible dimensions with less trouble than most of us imagine. We make an awful lot of trouble for ourselves in love, as in life, because of kneejerk prejudices, for or against. In the end, how much trouble love can contain without causing unbearable pain depends as much on a woman's understanding as it does on her emotions.

Of course there has to be a limit, there always is: a line beyond which understanding and loving acceptance turn into self-abasement, degradation and despair. Self-respect and self-preservation also set limits in this life and it is when they go beyond the boundaries of love that a woman who means to survive intact had better get out fast before all her emotions are engaged in a lost cause or enslaved to a dream of what is dead and gone.

'But I love him . . .' are words that depress my spirits, as in, 'He beats me, but I love him.' Or, 'He cheats on me, but I love him.' Or, 'He gambles away our rent money, but I love him . . .' And once, 'I came home and found him in bed with my mother, but I love him . . .'

When love becomes a burden — as soon as love needs to take a 'but' — it becomes a plaintive, long-suffering theme for old-fashioned torch-singers, and it ceases to be a manner or fashion of loving suitable to our time and our emergent feminine pride.

A woman writes, *'He never speaks to me except about what he wants to eat. We don't have sex any more. Sometimes he doesn't come home at night. But I love him. Don't tell me to leave him . . .'*

Practically without exception, when 'but I love him' letters come my way, they include the stipulation, 'Don't tell me to leave him.' Well, my friends, I'm afraid there is only room for one tyrant on an Agony column, and lots of times to leave him is precisely what I must say is in my opinion the smart thing to do, and the only thing. What is the alternative? Nag, scream, cry, beg, suffer, eventually come to blend your love utterly with pain, and then pass that unwholesome masochistic mess on to yet another generation of young women and agony aunts.

'No sexual activity between consenting adults that does not harm anyone can be ill-advised . . .' I remember writing those words back in the Seventies, and though I still hold to them in essence, I would now hedge them with caveats of middle-aged wisdom. For instance, not long after my liberal declaration, a mild element of sado-masochism slipped out of the esoteric into popular sexual activity. A noteworthy number of letters started arriving to do with bondage and spanking and fantasies of rape. I hold to the view that there's nothing 'wrong' with any of it: silk scarves and handcuffs are long-time sex toys, nineteenth-century Lords and Ladies spanked, and fantasies are fantasies are fantasies and nothing like facts. A shared taste for some spicy sado-masochism is not bad, bad, bad. Like shaving pubic hair or sex in the great outdoors, bondage and a bit of frisky slap and tickle add fun, fun, fun. However, when any special sexual activity ceases to be simply part of a repertoire and becomes obsessional, there are two points to consider: first, is it completely satisfying to but *one* of the partners? Is the other playing along, though bored to distraction, for the bad old reason of 'better the cock in hand . . .' — better to hang on to what she has because she's afraid to be alone? And second, is an obsessional repetitive sexual scenario in fact coming *between* the lovers and love? Is it expressing fear, in other words, of the very intimacy it parodies? And when it is, then surely it is not merely an erotic game, but a symptom of an underlying condition suitable for treatment.

A woman I've known as a friend for many years — I knew her when I wrote the 'anything goes' declaration — was so deeply attracted by sadistic sex on rather a cheerful level (involving 'naughty girls' and so forth) that she actually could not enjoy herself without a slipper or paddle nearby. She thought this was fine, why not? Everybody willing. Nobody hurt. And with the peculiarly naive egocentricity of people who have special sexual tastes, she assumed that all women, if they were brave enough to be honest, would agree that no sexual encounter was complete without some amicable slapping around. Inevitably, she attracted a series of men who wanted to play her game. Not one of her partners (truly the correct word in this context) lasted much more than a year or two, and not one of the five or six I have seen her with in all this time — not *one* — moved on to a happy relationship afterwards.

It seems to me now that the craving for exclusively sado-masochistic scenarios the men shared with my friend dramatised the fears and weaknesses of both parties and reinforced guilt which had no other outlet. Whenever they tried to make love, the compulsion to act out yet again what was bubbling away and troubling their deeper selves (though I have no doubt it ended in orgasms all around), was ultimately destructive of any hope for a lasting affair or marriage.

Modern lovemaking is pretty much detached from reproduction — if ten thousand couples in a town are making love on any given night, I dare say only two or three are actually trying for a baby — and it also reveals desires other than for affection and pleasure. Love is made out of vanity, too, out of fear of being alone, and sometimes out of a need for power. How we make love reflects and returns to our society at large more than just sexual energy. In the throes of sexual excitement, we rarely consider what we are actually doing, to ourselves as well as others, not physically perhaps, but on other levels of love. And life.

We think about sex all the time, but not much beyond how much we want it. That's why it is such a perplexing area of life. There is nothing 'wrong' with being absurdly sexy, by the by: it's the way we human animals are made. Coping with sexual desire pretty much on tap, however, justifying it to suit our moral code and adjusting it to 'love', puts a great strain on our hearts and minds and emotional resources.

Sexual intercourse has fashions, too. At the height of the Feminist movement back in the seventies, for example, letters used to arrive regularly either recommending or deploring the woman-on-top position in bed, as if it were a cultural barometer of urban communities, which in a way it was.

Lately, letters asking my views about three-in-a-bed have been arriving with increasing frequency, and it seems to me the practice is becoming a fad — though not yet a fashion. Whenever I receive a three-in-a-bed question, my impulse is against it. Because, yes, there are limits to what is sane and healthy, even in the name of love, and if three-in-a-bed reflects a response in men to a new and unfamiliar sense of powerlessness before a strengthened femalekind, as I dare say it does, then the problem is one that needs to be solved in practically every room of the house *other* than the bedroom where it is merely being acted out.

A woman writes, *'We've been together for nearly two years. Our sex life has been good. Now he says he'd like to bring another woman into the scene. He says it's up to me. The idea turns me on, but I'm scared to ruin what we have. Should I do it?'*

As hard as any one of us tries, she cannot be altogether without prejudices — nobody is that good. Knowing your prejudices and replacing them with as much understanding as you can is a lifetime job. A few prejudices are, however, based on practical evidence so there is good reason not to struggle too hard against them, at least not until the general climate we live in has altered and the facts have changed.

Is it not a fact, for example, that slavery is the most base institution of humankind and springs from our lowest impulses? If you disagree, then *you* tolerate it. I will not.

And whenever a lover brings another, male or female, into bed, it is *always* a power trip: to show how enslaved and obedient his woman (usually) is to his wishes. There are women (and men) who get a kick out of being manipulated by their partners, and there is love that can extend to utter debasement, à la *The Story of O*. But I can no more endorse ritualised humiliation as an expression of love than I could seriously recommend donning a collar and lead to trot ten paces behind Master to a dungeon party.

A woman writes, *'He says if I love him, I'll let him bring another woman into our lovemaking . . .'*
I reply, *'If he loved anyone other than himself he would not resort to blackmail. It takes two to make blackmail complete, by the way: perpetrator and victim.'*

'The idea turns me on a little . . .' is a frequent weak-kneed comment in letters about the threesome suggestion or requests for group sex.

So what if it does? Fantasies are a turn-on and some can be fun to en-act; not only are they sexy, but they make a sexy secret between a pair of lovers. But the best fantasies are effective because the sky is the limit. Drag a complex fanciful scenario down into the hard, solid world and, especially if it involves people other than the central couple, not only does it bring along danger and jealousy, in becoming real, it also loses its power as a fantasy and so must constantly be stoked to higher heat.

Once you agree to a threesome, in other words, there is no saying 'no' next time, and no going back, only forward into greater loss of privacy, intimacy and trust.

Yes, there exist couples who survive threesomes and group sex more or less intact; they are the exceptions. And take it from me, they have not written first to the Agony column for advice.

A woman writes, *'While on holiday I met a man I liked a lot, and I slept with him. He used a condom. Now I can't eat or sleep, I'm so terrified I might have caught AIDS. I would never have slept with someone so casually here.'*
I reply, *'AIDS is not a punishment. AIDS is not retribution. AIDS is a sexually transmitted disease and it must be approached as civilised people approach any disease. The chances of your having contracted AIDS from your liaison are very, very small. To set your mind at ease, go to your local STD clinic and have a simple blood test. A physical fact can be faced. It is superstition, guilt and panic that put us to shame.'*

All I need to do is suggest to a grown woman that she forgive her husband his infidelity, or forgive herself her own, and a torrent of letters take me to task for neglecting to mention what unforgivable selfishness it is in this day and age to risk passing on AIDS. Of course the danger is there and it's a virulent danger, too. And yes, disease is a risk and always has been, alleviated to some extent by the use of condoms. However, AIDS does not mitigate or change infidelity, say, or promiscuity, or alcohol-driven one night stands, nor does AIDS relieve us of the need to continue to think about these issues in terms of human emotions.

'Safe Sex' is very often a moraliser's euphemism for no sex at all. And there is no doubt that the safest sex is the least sex. Death, after all, is the ultimate contraceptive. But are we going to put a virus in charge of human passion and charity? Are we going to name a disease as our conscience? Moderation and common sense must surely be a more progressive, humane and far-sighted defence against every kind of illness than hysterical fulminations from the legion who can hardly wait to shout 'I told you so!' when all they ever told us was 'Don't!'

Love is not exactly what you want it to be, it's what you get. If you're lucky. And trouble comes when you think your love *should* be other than he is.

'Love is not love,' said the man who knew it all, 'which alters when it alteration finds . . .'

You name it, and somewhere, somehow, it is causing someone trouble in love. A great number of reasons for misery are self-inflicted, brought on by an attachment to the indisputably banal criteria which most of us use when we try to define what we think love *should* be, while at the same time we underestimate the moving, challenging, bemusing, relevant, sheltering, accepting, human thing love *can* be.

A woman writes, *'My boyfriend is twenty-four, and last week he had an erection in his sleep. How do I know he was dreaming of me? He says he can't remember. It's driving me crazy . . .'*
I reply, *'Give the guy a break. Maybe he was dreaming of you. Maybe he was dreaming of Hillary Clinton or the Queen. Maybe he was dreaming of a big pools win. Maybe he wasn't dreaming at all. Young men's cocks have dreams of their own. Erections happen. They are a physical response, not a barometer of emotions. No matter how deep love is, there are areas it cannot penetrate, some of them because they are too shallow — did love ever cure the common cold? Love may encourage erections but it can hardly be bothered to prevent one, especially in a man who is sound asleep.'*

Another woman writes, *'Last night when I was getting into the shower, I heard a noise. I looked out to see a figure on the roof. Suddenly, I had the sick realisation that it was my husband. He tried to deny it, but admitted he was trying to spy on me, and had done so before. I was numb with horror. He says it's because I never let him see my body . . .'*
I reply, *'Why not find ways to incorporate "peeping" into your sex life sometimes? Don't quite close the door when you bath . . . undress in front of a strategically placed mirror . . . There's no law against it in your own home. It will become a problem, however, if he is driven out into the neighbourhood to indulge his yen . . .'*

Still another writes, *'While cleaning out a boxful of junk in my lover's bookcase, I found poems he had written about a former girlfriend. We've been together for nearly a year now. They'd broken up a year before we met. He swore to me it was all finished with her. But why would he keep these poems if he didn't still think about her? I'm so hurt and angry . . .'*

I reply, *'He keeps the poems not because he remembers her, though of course he does remember her as I hope you remember every man who touched you deeply. He keeps the poems because he remembers himself as the kind of young lover who wrote poems. He's proud of his poems, on the sly. He would probably not be awfully pleased to know you have been snooping through his things, but I'll bet he'd like you to appreciate his romantic soul. So instead of attacking him about his 'ex', try talking to him about poetry. Better still, write him a poem. Play your cards right, in other words, and when he feels encouraged to write poems again, they will be for you.'*

Someone else writes, *'I love him very much but I don't think we're compatible. We live together. I love to shop on my days off, but he always wants to mooch around the house fixing things, or go out to football with his mates. He is being insensitive to my needs . . . I don't want to go on this way.'*

I reply, *'A bonus for little boys becoming big boys is that they no longer have to go shopping with mummy. You sound to me like a little girl trying to play house with a boy who'd rather not play. But this is not a game; it's the real thing. And if a grown man doesn't want to shop, for goodness' sake, why should he? Shop alone, and be happy he's there and that he's fixed the broken lamp when you get home. Otherwise, go ahead and break up, with my congratulations for having put forward the silliest reason I've come across.'*

When I started being an agony aunt, my impulse was always to assume all the flea-bites were symptoms of a deeper malaise. He didn't want to shop, let us say, because he resented her spending money he had earned, or money she had earned, etcetera, etcetera. And, yes, sometimes quibbles *are* the surface eruptions of something big, bad and deep. But I have discovered that as often as they symbolise or embody a deeper truth, they express nothing more than the immaturity of the writer, her exaggerated idea of what a man *should* be, her foggy vision of who the man in hand *is*, and her unreadiness for the give-and-take of live-in love.

A woman writes, *'My boyfriend and I are planning our wedding. Both my parents are elderly and my father had a heart attack a few years ago. He can't*

sleep at the thought of having to make a speech, so how will he cope on the
actual day? I am getting very stressed about this. My boyfriend doesn't seem
at all concerned. Am I making a mistake?'
I reply, *'Weddings are a celebration, not a drama. Just because the bride's*
father usually makes a speech does not mean the rule is carved in stone.
Someone else — an uncle or friend — could explain your father's allergy to
public speaking and propose a toast. Don't turn your wedding day into a
test . . .'

Most maddening to me, because they are least comprehensible, are
young women like this who can actually start to question their love
itself because of some point of protocol to do with their forthcoming
wedding. His mother drinks, for instance, and could make a scene at
the reception; her father drinks; her best friend's boyfriend doesn't
like the groom and so she says she won't be a bridesmaid; if her
mother's second husband attends, her natural father says he'll stay
away; his family *should* butt out because her family is paying. And if
her husband-to-be really loved her, he'd take her side.

Believe me, the list of wedding worries is as long as a society guest-
list. And the response that arises in me without fail is, 'Call the whole
thing off, then. Or elope.' It's a cry of sheer exasperation, an agony
aunt blowing off steam, and not of course what I write or recommend
after I've calmed down.

Weddings are, by the by, the *only* general area of complaint in
which I have not over the years had one single solitary letter from a
man. Why do you imagine that is?

'My wedding is the most important day of my life . . .' a young woman
writes inevitably.

First of all, I must say, if her wedding really is the most important
day she can look back upon or foresee, then she has not lived well
enough or long enough to know what she is talking about. Moreover, the use of the pronoun 'my', never 'our' — '*my* wedding . . .',
'*my* life' — stands as evidence of general ignorance of what lies
ahead. What lies ahead ? Marriage, for crying out loud.

A wedding is to marriage as a funeral is to death, only a wedding
precedes the greater happening. (When I was a kid, I preferred
funerals because nobody ever pointed to an open grave and said,
'Irma, you'll be next!') Why don't we do away with weddings once

and for all, on account of their expense and fussiness, if for no other reason. A dignified ceremony, plain clothes, a glass of champagne, and a few small gifts of money to start the couple on their way are surely all anyone needs to begin a happy marriage. The last thing true love wants is punctuation, and what is a wedding if not an elaborate exclamation mark? Or, just as often, a question mark! Besides, in the end weddings are too cute, too made just for women, reminiscent of the dowry system and with a terrible tendency towards 'daddy's-little-girlishness'. Down with them! What do you say? Let's not consider big, formal weddings a civilised way to celebrate an accord between two adult human beings. At least, not until the day a 'Groom's Shoppe' is to be found in every city where now there are only 'Bridal Shoppes'.

A woman writes, *'I married my husband six months ago. We had known each other ten months before that. He never gets out of bed. He cannot work. He had an illness before I met him and he needs to take all kinds of medication. The pills make him sick all the time. Doctors I have spoken to say they are not sure he will ever improve. I work day and night to keep us going. I'm still young and I want to leave him so I can have some kind of life. But how will he get along without me?'*

Sure, some men deliberately mislead or hide their flaws, so do women: a couple in love show only their best side to each other as a matter of course. And yes, there are conmen out there deliberately deceiving girls and collecting scalps. But where is the modern courtship carried out? Were these two, for example, on separate planets? His illness is not new, his incapacity to work could not just have started on their honeymoon. Was she so dazzled by love and the prospect of a husband that the effects of his medication were not evident to her soon after they met?

I hear from girls who married without any idea their new husbands had been in prison, say, or were bankrupts, or had an illegitimate child; others accepted a holiday Romeo to have and to hold without the slightest notion of how his family and friends were going to receive them, and often without any real knowledge of the man deeper than his big brown eyes, or sharper than their own adolescent daydreams. Love is blind, to be sure, and blinding. And love is deaf, and deafening. And I know love drives us crazy. But must love also make us stupid?

What *do* lovers talk about? *Do* lovers talk?

True, we marry for better or for worse, but is it not in our interests and the interests of our future children to have a pretty good idea of the odds before commitment? An alarming number of women find themselves hitched to inveterate gamblers, or junkies, or lechers, or drunks, and are surprised suddenly to see what must have been in front of their eyes all the time, clamouring for attention. Were they too befuddled by emotion to notice, until it was too late? Or did they imagine, poor things, that he'd change once they got him over the altar and home for keeps?

When I rule the world, I'm going to push through a law that allows couples in love to make love until the cows come home, but does not allow them to marry or have a child or sign a mortgage or commit themselves in any binding way before romantic and sexual passion have subsided a little and been tempered by acceptance and understanding. Women especially have a terrible weakness for romance: all it takes is a sniff of love to induce in us such stupefied lunacy that it is foolhardy not to say practically criminal to rush madly, blindly into a lifelong contract and start a whole new line in human beings until the fit has passed. Ideally, then, no woman would ever again join forces with a man because she could not live without him; they'd move in together only when she was sure she could live *with* him. It's a nice idea and it would certainly help ease us agony aunts into early retirement.

Take the subject of ex-wives, for example. Virtually any man who has been married before (and according to our divorce rate there are lots and lots of them) will have an ex-wife. She must be included in the equation to whatever degree she still intrudes in his life: one and one, in other words, *has* been known to make three. Or four. Or more. Some ex-wives are holy terrors. Before a couple start living together, the machinations of a flaky 'ex' can seem kind of cute. 'You poor darling, how you must have suffered with that witch! And have you noticed how much sweeter I am than her?' But after the knot has been tied or the mortgage papers signed? Easy though it is to love him, to love the baggage that comes with him can put a strain on any woman's emotional capacity. So why are so many so dazed and deluded *before* they commit themselves, that not very long afterwards they have to write to an agony aunt like me, in wretched surprise at the goings on of an 'ex' who was there all along?

And it's no good saying 'He *should* have told me!' There are some things a girl has to figure out for herself.

A woman writes, *'His ex-wife is on the phone every week asking him to do things like pick the kids up after school. She even called him once to change a light bulb. They were married for fifteen years. Can't she understand he's with me now?'*
I reply, *'She was his dependant for fifteen years. And she never asked for her freedom, did she? Independence is bound to be hard and find her utterly unprepared. Be patient. And be warned by her example not to let yourself ever become so totally dependent that you are helpless on your own . . .'*

'Brace yourself' is usually the best I can say on the subject of a rampaging 'ex', though bracing is a whole lot better done before rather than after the fact. And plan a strategy: two telephones? An answering machine to screen all calls? A guard-dog? Life in another country or state? And above all, whatever gritting of your teeth is necessary, maintain a dignified and united front with your husband or lover, until the maddened 'ex' realises she really is outnumbered and gives up the fight.

A woman writes, *'His five-year-old spends every other weekend with us. He gives her anything she wants and whatever she wants to do takes precedence over my wishes. It just isn't fair. How long should I put up with it?'*
I reply, *'You will have to put up with it until the child grows up. Or you do.'*

When he has a child or children from a former union, if you accept him wholly, you have no choice but to include the part of him that is forever them. Whenever a grown-up (you) pits herself against a child (his) it's an ugly business, for no matter how dreadfully behaved the brat, you can take it as read that he or she is more confused and hurt by the breakup at home than you, or anyone, even his 'ex'. Woo the child, win the child, learn to enjoy the child. Remember, unlike adults, children change from day to day, they can be influenced, and sometimes they improve.

Letters arrive, about a dozen times a month, moaning about problems with a lover's kids, and I always ask the writer if she would love him more if he were the sort of man who could abandon the offspring of his previous relationships? If her answer could be 'yes', then let her not consult this agony aunt and tempt me to the sin of 'I told you so' later, when her light-minded grasshopper abandons *her*.

Judging from my post-bag, exes and their kids are at around number six, about neck in neck with in-laws, on the 'top ten' of problems that people in love help to make for themselves.

A woman writes, *'I am married to a man I love with all my heart. The problem is his parents, especially his mother. She is constantly calling us, sometimes three and four times a day. I don't dislike her, but I feel they expect too much of our time . . . and they make us feel guilty because they have done a lot for us. They bore me . . . they are completely annoying. My mother-in-law is always dropping hints about my weight . . . she has more of a weight problem than I do. She is also constantly reminding me she wants grandchildren even when she knows we aren't ready for them. Why can't they be more like my parents?'*

As is often the case with complaints of this kind, the writer is lying; what's more, she is lying to that most vulnerable victim of any liar — herself. She *does* dislike her in-laws, especially her mother-in-law. Of course, she thinks she *shouldn't*, but every word of her letter shows she dislikes the hell out of them. And until she admits she dislikes them, she will continue futilely complaining that they *should* change — 'Why can't they be more like my parents?' — instead of applying herself to the only real hope, which is to change how she feels about them. Until she admits to herself she dislikes them, there is no way she can learn to like them, or even to tolerate them with good grace.

In western society, a mother-in-law does *not* become her daughter-in-law's surrogate mother. Nevertheless, the language of most of the letters complaining of a mother-in-law or a boyfriend's mother makes it all too clear that the writer has cast her in the role of her own mother, and so anticipates all the old troubles she had as a child, and to anticipate trouble is uncomfortably close to asking for it. The daughter-in-law is behaving like a kid again, in other words, and therefore has put herself in no position to win the battle if her mother-in-law turns out to be a bad one.

What is a bad mother-in-law? A son who is unwilling or unable to free himself from mama's apron-strings is enough to give any sensible woman serious reason for concern *before* she commits herself to him. Mama's boys make chilly lovers and bad long-term mates. By the same token, the bad mother-in-law is the one who cannot let her son go without a fight. She loved him first, after all, and to whatever degree she is a possessive mama, his new wife or girlfriend is automatically 'the other woman'. More often than not, a bad mother-in-law has been regularly disappointed by the men in her life, and she clings all the harder, therefore, to the last man left to her: her son. And in a sense, she really *has* lost him to another woman.

A mother-in-law has no real power whatsoever in the new household, only what she can bully out of the other woman, her daughter-in-law. But remember, the bad mother-in-law feels herself to be the woman scorned, so just let her see how easy it is to get under her successful rival's skin and she will gleefully do it again, and again, and endlessly, until at last the daughter-in-law recognises how pathetic the old girl really is, uses her head, and smiles.

In the usual course of things, a mother-in-law is considerably older than the girl her son decides to live with, but that does not mean a wise daughter-in-law can't apply some useful tips from 'child psychology' when dealing with her. In short, never let the old bag see she is getting to you.

When mum-in-law tries to sting with insults about her son's wife's weight, say, or her cooking, or her reluctance to start a family right away, it really is no more significant than an old vaudeville joke, *unless* the daughter-in-law is so insecure in herself, of course, and such a child before a mother — *any* mother — that she cannot laugh down feeble barbs, or turn them diplomatically aside. If the younger woman can smile, if she can talk sensibly, if she can grow up enough to understand a little the feelings of the older woman, then big mama will have to give up, disarmed. And who knows? From newly established vantage points, they can even start to like each other. Stranger things have happened.

Guilt prevents many women admitting they dislike their in-laws. I mean, nice people *shouldn't* dislike people of their parents' age, *should* they? Chances are their son dislikes them too, but only imagine what guilt it will produce in *him* if his girlfriend or wife tries to set him up against his very own mum and dad? When a girlfriend or wife nags a man to ally himself with her and against his family, she is asking for trouble and playing right into the hands of a bad mother-in-law, who sees herself, remember, as the first and primary woman in her son's life.

Patterns begin slowly and are hard to break once they are established; a smart daughter-in-law who is not acting out her own childhood grabs control of the pattern of her meetings with in-laws as soon as the ink is dry on the marriage licence. Instead of waiting for them to invite her, or themselves, for example, she invites them at spaced and regular intervals: one dinner every two weeks, say. If she makes it a festive occasion, they will have no reason to complain of neglect (which is not to say they won't complain anyway).

If a girl thinks her own parents set an example of what good in-laws can be, she can mix them up together sometimes. And when her in-laws invite her back, every other time or so she will have an *honest* excuse not to go, so they get the idea of how busy the new couple is.

Children have every reason to assume that anything generous and good their in-laws or parents do for them, they do out of genuine love. Loans must be repaid in kind, of course. But the only repayment for gifts is warmth in the heart of the giver. When parents do expect something intangible, like affection or obedience, in exchange for financial help, say, or other favours, then they have not really *given* at all: they have tried to *buy*, and their children are perfectly entitled to refuse the terms.

So many troubles in love, you see, are homemade and created by our own bedazzled selves. Money causes as much stress in unions as infidelity, for instance, yet even as I write these words there are women out there about to throw their lot in with men whose economic status is vague and who have not discussed with him how they will manage their joint finances.

How unromantic can Aunt Irma be? As unromantic as mortgages, repayments on a car, legal fees, food, rent, and all the other worldly thorns that will make trouble tomorrow for today's love, unless women have the sense to bring them out into the open and factor them into their commitment.

Have pity for 'In Pain'! Alarming, isn't it, all that her relatively straightforward problem has stirred up in one agony aunt? If she could get inside my head as I read her letter, I bet she'd regret ever coming to me for my opinion. Then again, by the time I'd finished my tirade, she could have forgotten what her problem was and why she wrote to the Agony column in the first place. And do you know? That would be no bad thing.

● ● ● ● ● ● ● ● ● ●

Dear 'In Pain',

   Lovemaking slows down in relationships. It would have to, wouldn't it, or nothing else would ever get done. But when it drops to the point where one of the lovers needs more, there is a problem. Assuming your boyfriend is in good health, the cause of his sexual lethargy could, as you have suggested, be the scary responsibility of starting his own business. A tired, distracted man is not likely to be in the mood for great extended lovemaking. By the way, when you say he rises to the occasion only once a week 'if you're lucky', I assume you have tried making some luck of your own. Slow, sensual, seductive caresses could help relax him: massage, for example, and moves more voluptuous than aggressively sexy. With all he has to worry about at work, relaxation at home would be a whole lot sexier than arousal which, like it or not, he may be getting, short and sharp and simple, from his little collection of porn.

   Mind you, it is equally likely he's forgotten all about the girlie magazine and porn video you found. Have you thought they could matter a lot more to you than they do to him? Sometimes porn can be a problem, yes, but I suspect it is not one in your case, and I hope you do not let it distract you from your lover's wellbeing, or your own. Could you possibly cheerfully share his sexy mag and video? Don't even try if the idea repels you. But one way or another you will eventually have to bring what you found out into the open because it is secretly bothering you. Solitary distress is infinitely more destructive to a loving union than a little solitary masturbation.

   Bear in mind that confrontation can be worse than silence and more troubling to your mutual understanding unless you set about it with genuine concern and affection. Whenever two people square off for a fearless heart-to-heart, they must both be prepared calmly to hear things they would rather not know. High-pitched accusations do more harm than good, they lead to overstatement in the heat of anger, and they drive men, who do not as a rule take to scenes, into a corner or out the door. So calm down, find or create an atmosphere of quiet trust, and talk to him about his deeper self, his worries, and incidentally, if you need to, about the porn you found.

Go in peace,
Irma

• • • • • • • • • •

AGONY AUNT'S WORKSHEET

1. If pornography is 'bad'
   a. Is it *always* bad?
   b. If a man is turned on by it is he a 'bad' man?
   c. If a woman is turned on by it, is she 'bad'?
   d. If a couple enjoy it in the privacy of home are they 'bad' people?
2. *Can* there be love without trouble?
3. What are the problems you have known yourself or observed in the marriages and love affairs of others, starting with the *least* urgent?
4. Do you believe that for *every* problem in love there is always a fair solution — I mean a solution that does not require either lover to surrender self-esteem, hope or principles to the other lover?
5. Is love more important than self-esteem, hope and principles?
6. Name what is left of love if you take away one partner's self-esteem or hope. Start with the *most* important.
7. How would you answer 'In Pain's' letter?

PROBLEM FIVE

What are the odds of happiness with a married man?

•••••••••

Dear Irma,

    I'm twenty-five years old. Last year I met the man of my dreams. He's sensitive, caring, he earns good money, and he is a great lover. The only trouble is, he's married. Friends say she is spiteful, always trashing her husband and saying hurtful things about him. They have no love-life at all any more — he only stays in the marriage for his two children. They are ten and thirteen. Don't tell me to drop him because I love him. All I want is to be with him for the rest of my life.

The 'Other Woman'

•••••••••

I've given a lot of thought to monogamy. Having never signed up for it, I have probably thought about it more than those who take it for granted as a way of life. And I have started to think that our kind of romantic monogamy, one man and one woman, is the luxury product of an established, relatively successful race. It's hard to imagine that our prehistoric ancestors, for instance — one male, one female — spotted each other in the gloom and knew across the crowded cave they were meant for each other alone, to have and to hold, as long as they both were to live — around nineteen years, I believe. Even Adam and Eve, if you hold with the tale, though indisputably made for each other, had no say-so in the matter and less choice than anyone ever since. Romantic love, one-on-one love — love-love — is not a God-given right, in other words, and once the Garden of Eden was behind our founding couple, love's history became as problematical as the history of any conquest or war.

In the dark primeval night, humankind must have been driven to mate by an innate urge to ensure the survival of their species rather than any yen for our kind of exclusive, monogamous lovemaking which, at the very least, loves a little privacy. Caveman probably fell for cavewoman, or more likely for cavewomen in general, because the female contained babies, and babies were the future. And cavewoman cleaved unto the best mate she could attract for as long as he brought home the bacon, thus giving their offspring a better chance to survive and pass their wilful, overbearing genes down to succeeding generations.

We ought to be grateful our distant forebears managed without the mushy stuff till death them did part. If they had spent their time in single courtships followed by exclusive unions, far fewer young would have been born to outlive them, and chances are the 'Other Woman' would not be here now, nor her lover, nor his wife, nor anybody. Other animals couple under the blind imperative of continuing their line; they are driven to breed as they are to feed or breathe, by tyrannical life itself, and not by what we call 'love'. When times were hard and our pre-eminence in the history of the world was less certain, why should we have been any different from other competitive lifeforms?

We *can* live without monogamy. We *can* live without love. Only we'd really rather not. Love for us is very like music and art; it probably began as a mystical service. To paint a gazelle on the rock face, for instance, was to offer up a prayer more magical than words for what the hunter most desired. And over the ages, his primitive appeals to unknown powers became increasingly complex and beautiful: they became cathedrals, and portraits that outlived the sitter, and other marvellous abstractions. Why shouldn't the way we love be like the way we make art and music? — derived from heart-felt prayer for a soulmate and an end to loneliness.

That I honestly conclude monogamous love to be our own invention does not mean I hold it in contempt, you see. On the contrary, the ideal of sexual fidelity is our hearts' own, and the very fact that we instituted marriage in a spirit of hopefulness and in the main for the best seems to me all the more reason to cherish the institution and treat it with respect.

We may not need exclusive monogamy, is what I'm saying, but it is beautiful, we *want* it, and it works in principle, so even those of us who choose not to participate in it are dutybound to keep it in good health.

Okay, I know our love rarely lives up to expectations, it is everywhere being debased, and often it causes pain. But surely that is all the more reason why every couple brave enough to enter into a contract of exclusive loving have a responsibility to do their best to behave with kindness and honour, if only so others will say, 'True enough, it doesn't often work. But it is working for them.'

'Responsibility' is not taken awfully seriously; it is certainly not up there with 'love' and 'success' and 'happiness'; it doesn't pop up nearly as often as 'rights', at least not in the letters I read. Ask ten young women (men, too, I expect) what they want most of all from life and if even one of them replies, 'lots and lots of responsibility', this agony aunt will eat her hat. But there is no love or success without responsibility, nor can there be lasting happiness without it.

Why am I preparing to lace into the 'Other Woman' this way? Surely it has to be the married man who has all the duties and responsibilities? Of course it is. But that does not absolve the 'Other Woman' from *her* responsibilities, nor me from mine, come to that.

The 'Other Woman' has presented me with what is to some degree a moral issue because it is concerned not merely with emotions, but just as much with the institutions of our world. As long as an agony aunt holds no doctrinaire line — I cannot, for example, simply tell her, 'Thou shalt not . . . and there's an end to it!' — she has to continue to think her way into a moral issue every time one of them crops up. Problems of this nature are solved from the top down, and even the least judgemental agony aunt must keep clarifying where she stands generally on the whole area of, say, adultery, before she looks at the specific case in front of her and weighs up the chances that it is exceptional.

Adultery is not nice. And an adulterous partner is rarely a candidate for security in love, if that is what the 'Other Woman' is looking for. Of course, there do exist husbands, and wives too, whose spouses have become so much less than was bargained for originally that it would be inhumane to demand lifetime fidelity. But it's my impression that there are far, far fewer Mr Rochesters in this life, and loony wives raving in towers, than exist in novels and old movies.

In all my decades as an observer of things going on around me, and later as an agony aunt, I've come upon perhaps two cases of what might qualify as 'justifiable adultery': one where the husband was a rogue, mostly in gaol or in flight, and the other where a woman was so pathologically jealous she used to cut her lover's clothes into shreds to prevent him going out at night. Extremes like that, I guess, could justify adultery. The funny thing is, both the put-upon halves of these couples were faithful as rocks. But that's another problem.

As for 'adultery in the second degree', when his (or her) life at home is so unpleasant and the contracted mate so cold or fiendishly awful that adultery must be at least understandable, I suppose this happens a great deal more often than undeniably 'justifiable' adultery. However, the 'Other Woman' is the last person to be in a position to judge the true nature of her lover's adultery, for she hears only half the story: his half.

'Friends say she is spiteful . . .' Whose friends, I wonder? Friends of the 'Other Woman', I guess. Love is obsession, and because she is obsessed, she probably provokes her friends into talking about her beloved at every chance she gets. And then the 'Other Woman's' friends are bound to oblige her by saying whatever she wants to hear because, after all, they like her and hope to make her feel good. Besides, as often as not, they will say anything to shut her up at last so they can all talk about something other than her married lover for a change!

Friends make bad spies. They have an investment in the outcome and lack the detachment necessary for non-judgemental note-taking.

Anyhow, the 'Other Woman' is not really hearing what her friends tell her, only making them repeat themselves over and over on the topic of 'him' until, if only in desperation, they come up with something she wants to hear, whereupon she will make them repeat *that* over and over and over again, until the words lose all sense except whatever her wishful thinking manages to make of them.

A woman writes, *'They have no love-life any more. He told me their marriage was a big mistake. He says he is going to leave his wife. But he can't just now because their first baby is due in five months . . .'*

I do not need a degree in mathematics to know that a mere four months ago, this man and his wife were going at it, right? And the girl who loves him adulterously hardly needs to have studied psychology to suspect that a man whose wife is pregnant with their first baby could be feeling worried, endangered, and in need of comfort for a while, especially if he himself is barely out of diapers. But love keeps a different clock from common sense, and of all lovers except first-time lovers, those who engage in love extra-maritally seem the least analytical and the most deluded.

One of my dear friends is a cancer specialist, and I once trailed along the wards behind her for a few days while I was researching a book on death and dying.

'Are you the kind of person who likes to know everything that is happening?' she asked one middle-aged man.

'Oh yes, doctor,' he said, and sat up straighter in his tartan robe. 'Certainly, I am.'

She then told him gently and clearly, without frills, that his condition was very, very serious, possibly fatal, and that the treatment he was about to start was going to make him very ill and tired.

'I see,' he said, and he smiled winningly. 'But you'll have me fit to go skiing next month, won't you?'

Love, too, is a mortal's condition, though not usually mortal, and a devastatingly self-interested censor bleeps out what it does not care to know.

'They have no love-life any more . . .' How, pray, does the 'Other Woman' know this fact? (And I've yet to receive a letter from 'Another Woman' who does *not* say that she knows her married lover's home-life is on the rocks.) She knows because he told her, that's how. How else? And how, I wonder, does the 'Other Woman' define a 'love-life'. Not the same way he does, I'll wager.

If he and his wife still share a bed, a room, a house, they are bound to touch and now and again to catch a glimpse of what once upon a time drove them wild about each other: they will be turned on, in short, and then make the most of what by law and habit and convention is not only permissible, but expected of married people. For him, such encounters may be comfortably familiar, plain and simple, and hardly chart-topping on the scale of excitement. When he tells the 'Other Woman', 'My old lady and I don't have a love-life any more,' he means it in his own terms. But the 'Other Woman' would be appalled to know that when her married lover says he has no love-life with his wife, he does not necessarily mean they have no sex.

And what about his wife or live-in girlfriend? Chances are the passing sexual contacts, possibly occurring quite regularly, are for her too something more like a love-life than not. Moreover, it is not unknown for an errant husband to be sexier than usual at home, not simply to cover his tracks, but because sneaking around creates a state of perpetual excitement in some men.

A woman writes, *'We broke up ten months ago. I know he's seeing someone else. But we still have sex whenever we meet; down deep he must still love me . . .'*
I reply, *'As long as you continue to make love with a man, you may be his "ex", but he is not yours, and you have to begin getting over him again every time he leaves your bed.'*

I'm struck over and over again by how the female sex equates two vital four-letter words that have not so much as one letter in common — 'love' and 'fuck' — and over and over again I find myself wondering if 'Someone Else' has any notion whatsoever that her lover is betraying her, for that is how she would see it, with his 'ex' girlfriend, or his estranged wife.

I am nobody's fool, as a rule, but the only time (so far as I know) that I was being two-timed I hadn't a clue, until under pressure from his reactivated 'ex', my lover 'confessed' all, to my utter astonishment. 'When did you find the time?' I cried.

Sex and love are commingled so exquisitely in us women that a love affair or marriage is never over, not in the heart or mind of the human female at least, until the lovemaking has ended altogether.

There is no point trying to get over him, as so many who write to me say they are trying to do, if you continue to sleep together, even only on birthdays and high holidays, for every time he leaves your bed, be it at midnight or at dawn, you will have to set out once again on the long, hard road of wishful thinking and getting over him.

To make love again with a man who has left you and is your 'ex' in all but body is as if you chose to tread water in the path of a shark, instead of swimming clean out of his way.

A woman writes, *'I don't want it to happen. I don't approve of love with married men. But the idea of sex with him is irresistible . . .'*

Curiosity is an element in every new sexual encounter. The trouble is it isn't satisfied as easily as an itch. 'Irresistible sex' is not something a woman works out of her system in a few hours, then shakes hands and says, 'See you around.' She may think she can do it before the act, and no doubt there are some cool cookies who do sometimes walk away unscathed (I have in my time) but not after every encounter — one is bound to get to her in the end. And the thousands who have written to me over the years have indubitably been got to by what they say they thought was going to be a passing encounter.

I am not referring here to a frivolous or drunken one night stand, of course (that's another problem), but attraction to a man who appears often enough to set a woman daydreaming about 'irresistible sex' with him. A lot of unsuccessful marriages have been based on irresistible sexual attraction. And I imagine relatively successful infidelities could be based on the same thing: successful to the degree, I mean, that the adulterous couple have a great time in bed every so often, with no harm done to anyone, I guess (I have my doubts). Unless, of course, love moves on in with 'irresistible sex', as nine times out of ten it appears to do, certainly as far as women are concerned.

Sexual attraction, as we agony aunts say *ad nauseam*, loses its blaze in the day-to-day exercise of marriage, and settles into something more warm than hot. But in a thrilling catch-as-catch-can affair, the sex goes on sizzling longer. Why? For one reason, because it comes attached to no chilling responsibilities. In other words, sex with a married man is irresistible sex for some women precisely because it is irresponsible sex, which is great, as long as they can swear hand on heart that they will never ever want more than that.

Or is it all that great? And is there really no harm done by a merry no-strings infidelity? If the betrayed wife is unhappy, or if she does not understand her husband's new coolness, or if she intuits something bad that she cannot quite name or prove, then the 'Other Woman' is in the unenviable position of being an accomplice in the cause of another woman's pain. Is it ever possible to build any kind of happiness on the suffering of another? If you believe it is, then go ahead and try. For my part, I doubt it. Call it fanciful, but sadness seems to me to cling to any affair that is causing pain to someone else; sadness, or a febrile excitement, which is surely no more wholesome or hopeful or happy for extra-marital lovers.

Then again, if his wife really is altogether in the dark about the existence of the 'Other Woman', the odds are he is one of those husbands whose infidelities make him more charming and ardent at home out of guilt, or fear of discovery. Not something the 'Other Woman' wants to know; not something he's going to want to tell her, I dare say. But in a sense it is the 'Other Woman', as well as the wife, who is being shortchanged.

In either case, whether a husband hurts his wife with his adultery or blinds her with increased attention and affection, the prognosis for the 'Other Woman' is not so hot. Unless, of course, due to a fluke of her personality, she actually prefers her private life to be theatrical and irresponsible, in which case you can be sure she is a good deal older than the 'Other Women' who generally consult me; she has something solid going for her in her work, or some other area of her life; she never cries on friends' shoulders or writes to agony aunts; she probably keeps a poodle — or a rottweiler. And I wouldn't be surprised if she is not American or Anglo-Saxon.

There are societies reputedly more pragmatic than ours where a husband's infidelity is said to be accepted pretty much as a matter of course. And there are sophisticated big cities where infidelity on both sides is supposed to be tacitly acceptable. Here and there, there still exist 'mistress cultures' with women, practically a separate class of them, ready to play the traditional 'Other Woman' role. But don't believe everything you hear or read on the topic, especially if it has been put about by the men. The wives I know to be most ground down and distressed by their husbands' macho meanderings off the marital path are all from Central and Latin American countries. And the only woman I've ever known to go half mad with mortification, when her husband quite discreetly took a mistress, was a Parisian.

'All I want is to be with him,' writes the 'Other Woman'. And the word 'happiness' flits round the edge of her letter like the will o' the wisp it is. Is there hope for happiness if it is based on 'all she wants', which is 'to be with him', presumably for ever? Everyone knows of a few second marriages between husbands, once adulterous, and the 'Other Women' they were fooling around with, and even though second and third marriages have an equally high disaster rate, good luck to them! Why not?

But for every 'Other Woman' who has got her man, agony aunts know dozens more left in the lurch by him as soon as his home-life took a turn for the better. And others who woke up at forty-odd and were *still* the 'Other Woman'. And many many more than you imagine who rejoiced when he left his wife at last, only to be immediately broken-hearted to see him waltz off into the sunset with a woman other than themselves.

I genuinely believe the 'Other Woman' who wants happiness with a married man had better be prepared to base it on whatever time he has to spare for her, when he has time to spare, and for as long as he can spare it. Having 'Another Woman' is a sort of power trip for any man and there is something weak and clinging in the position of the women, wife and mistress both, who put up with it.

Except for cases so rare I cannot recall them, so remote I cannot find them in my files, I have never seen any reason to encourage the 'Other Woman' or suggest strategies to get her lover out of his original oath or contract. Admittedly, whenever the 'Other Woman' writes to me, my heart and mind go out to the *other* woman, the one who does actually have some rights in the business, the one who generally wins him back, damaged though he may be, in the end.

In brief, the cards are stacked against the 'Other Woman'. And when things do not work out for her in the long run, she will not even have the dubious right of an ex-wife to blame the bastard who started all the trouble in the first place.

• • • • • • • • • •

Dear 'Other Woman',

You tell me what not to tell you: I must not tell you to leave him. Why not? Because you love him. Thus, I assume that as far as you are concerned love comes before everything else in this life, including truth and honour and happiness. Because the truth is that the chances of happiness with a married man who is in bad faith with his spouse are not terrific.

Do you know why some women actually prefer to be, like you, the 'Other Woman', and not his resident mate? Precisely because they do not love the man, that's why. They miss him. They want him. The thought of him prevents (protects?) them from looking anywhere else for love. But they do not love him. They do love the attention, the drama, the romantic evenings, the sneaky trips; they love the suffering, they love his desperate lies. They love being securely irresponsible. They mind being alone on Christmas and their birthdays, but they do not mind at all sending him home in dirty socks for his wife to wash. But if you were made as successful mistresses are, you wouldn't be writing to me, would you? You want this man, dirty socks and all. So I won't suggest that you leave him now, while you are young and still open to offers. What would be the use? You have already told me what not to tell you. And you wouldn't hear me anyhow. Because you have not written to hear what I hold true; you want me to send you a magic potion by return post that will make him leave his wife. But I'm afraid there has been a run on that particular brand of medicine and I'm all out of it.

I'll tell you simply to relish every hour he is free to spend with you, in case they are all you will have, which is more than likely. And I'll tell you not to expect or demand more from him than he is

*already giving you. And I'll tell you to be prepared for a whole lot
less than you want from life with a man.*

Regretfully,
Aunt Irma

• • • • • • • • • •

AGONY AUNT'S WORKSHEET

1. What is the difference between happiness and the
   pursuit of happiness?
2. Where do rights come from?
3. Can there exist a right without a responsibility? If you
   think so, name three.
4. Does anyone have the right to cause unhappiness to
   another or others in her (or his) own rightful *pursuit* of
   happiness? By what authority is the right to cause pain
   granted and guaranteed?
5. Is it possible to have an affair with another woman's
   husband without hoping or dreaming his marriage will
   break up?
6. An unfaithful husband is in bad faith with his wife, but
   if he continues to make love to her and treat her well, is
   he also in bad faith with the Other Woman?
7. How many sides has every story of adultery? One, two,
   three, or more?
8. Write a reply to the 'Other Woman'.

PROBLEM SIX

Is infidelity ever forgivable?

• • • • • • • • • •

Dear Irma,

I thought I was a happily married woman. My husband and I lived together for two years and have been married for just over two years. A few months ago, I found a letter in the pocket of a suit I was sending to the cleaners. It was from another woman and it was clear there was something between them. When I told him, he said he loved me, and it was all over with the other woman; she was never important to him and it had only happened twice with her. He swears it was all a mistake. He cried, and I forgave him. We agreed not to mention it again. But now every time he touches me, I think about what he did, and I feel so hurt. I only want things to be the way they were.

'Betrayed'

• • • • • • • • • •

Friendship is an ideal. Love itself is an ideal. Fidelity in love and marriage is an ideal. Ideals lift our noses out of the feeding trough, and whatever trouble they get us into, we'd be lost without them. Three-quarters of the letters about infidelity that come my way are from women writing out of deep despair when someone *else*, a man generally, has failed to live up to the ideal they were pledged to share. Sometimes, it must be said, the ideal of fidelity is ludicrously exaggerated.

A woman writes, *'My boyfriend and I had a break so he could be sure about "us". Then he called round, saying how much he missed me. The problem is that in the weeks prior to this a family friend had taken me out. My boyfriend found out and was surprisingly understanding. He then admitted that while we were apart he had taken a girl out for a drink. He says he is sorry but I cannot forgive him. I told him I never wanted to see him again . . .'*

I reply, *'Your letter comes from another century. Loving each other does not condemn us to become each other's slaves. When women struggled for equality (and I hope they still do), it was not so that men could join us in the exclusive prison where we used to live most of our lives. For goodness' sake, tell him you're sorry for acting like a warden instead of a friend . . .'*

About a quarter of my letters on the topic of infidelity are from women who have themselves been unfaithful.

A woman writes, *'After nearly ten years of marriage, I've fallen in love with a man I worked with for some time . . .'*

Another writes, *'You may not think being unfaithful is such a dreadful thing in this day and age, but I'm finding it traumatic . . . I have an adorable baby and I always thought I loved my husband . . . I have a strict religious background and I have fallen in love with a man I met in the church choir . . .'*

Still another, *'After ten years of marriage, I've fallen in love with a man I work with . . .'*

And, *'My boss is everything I ever wanted in a man. I still love my husband, but . . .'*

Whenever journalists contact me in my capacity as an agony aunt for quotes to flesh out their lurid surveys of sexual harassment in the workplace, I have to disappoint them. I'm afraid I haven't much evidence to support their preconceptions of white slavery among the nine-to-fivers. It's love in the office, not management-level lechery, that seems to predominate in my postbag.

Evidently pashas knew what they were doing when they locked their harems: it seems that female fidelity can depend as much upon opportunity (or rather the lack of it) as upon our vaunted superior idealism in matters of romance. More often than not, the infidelities I hear about are taking place with a man at work. But it isn't just the workplace that provides temptation. There are other 'arenas of availability', too — within the community or even within the family — and these figure in women's infidelities more often than I would have imagined before I became an agony aunt.

A woman writes, *'I am having sex with my boyfriend's brother. I feel bad, but I love him . . .'*

Another says, *'My father-in-law and I have started a sexual relationship. I still love my husband in a way, but his father is a sensational, exciting man . . .'*

And, *'My sister's husband and I are lovers. I tried to resist but I couldn't. She'll kill me if she finds out. I love him. I'm pregnant . . .'*

Obviously, a woman locked up at home has far fewer opportunities to meet available men. But, given the chance, women in the calm shallows of a long marriage or live-in affair seem almost as eager as men to fall off the faithful wagon, although they do it less often and less lightheartedly, or so it seems from my side of the postbag. Men still have more opportunity for infidelity. Also the nature of women's desire is not exactly the same as his. And finally, women may have children to consider.

When I identify and describe what I've noticed about sexual differences in the matter of infidelity, it is not because I'm a turncoat feminist, nor have I suddenly become anti-egalitarian. The evidence I see and cannot deny is that adulterous women are not the same as adulterous men, just as there is inequality in many areas of villainy. (Have you noticed, by the by, how rarely women are at the centre of big financial scams?) But maybe if we keep trying, sisters, maybe someday we will be the equal of our brothers in betrayal.

Remorse and guilt seem in general to torture adulterous men: they sure as hell torture the ones who have been found out. Guilt bothers unfaithful women too, of course, but what troubles most of those who write to me is, above all, love. Unlike 'Betrayed's' husband, a betraying wife can very rarely say her affair was unimportant; at least she very rarely says it to me. Almost every unfaithful woman who comes my way is torn between the man at home and the Other Man.

A woman writes, *'I am twenty-six, living for five years with a man who is kind and loving. There is another man about whom I care. I love him, too. I don't want to hurt anyone but I feel I must explore more of life . . .'*

Another says, *'Ten months ago I was married but there is a lack of sexual interest on my husband's side. He makes me feel so unwanted. Meanwhile, I've met this guy at work and there is something so strong between us. I'm falling in love with him. We haven't had sex yet, but I know we will . . .'*

And, *'I am thirty, married for eleven years to my first boyfriend, with three lovely children. I get along tolerably well with my husband. We are relatively happy. For the past two years I have known a salesman who comes into the office where I work. He fills the emotional gaps my husband leaves . . .'*

Love and sex are yoked perpetually, if uneasily, in the imagination of a whole lot of modern women — even more so now, I dare say, than in the old days when love between a man and woman was widely expected to be marital, and marital sex was a duty. There are mornings when my postbag is unusually tear-stained and blue, and I have to wonder if Women's Liberation did not set a generation of females free alright, straight into the deep purple landscape of a romantic pulp novel.

Love, as far as a great many women are concerned, even in this day and age of nearly equal opportunity and equal responsibility, is the great absolving balm that heals and excuses everything, including lechery, treachery, stupidity and selfishness.

A woman writes, *'We don't want to hurt his wife and children, but we love each other . . .'*

Another writes, *'He is serving a prison sentence for a violent crime. My parents hate him. But all that matters is I love him . . .'*

And, *'My sister will be upset when she finds out her boyfriend and I are meeting secretly. But the love between us is too strong to resist . . .'*

'My brother and I have been lovers for five years, since I was seventeen and

97

he was eighteen. Nothing could be more perfect than the way we feel about each other. Now I am pregnant . . .'

And again, *'He's forty-three, I'm seventeen. How can I make him stop worrying about the age difference? Love doesn't tell time . . .'*

I reply, *'Don't kid yourself. In the end, time tells love and everything else just where to get off.'*

Many young women tend to believe that love will always kiss it better, certainly as long as they are on the receiving end. Yet the truth of the matter is that not always, but often enough to matter, when a woman's infidelity is causing her pain, it is not really due to love at all, but to love's downfall: her adulterous lover is very often, more than he is anything else, a way to flee the failure of love at home.

The adultery a woman brings to my attention is frequently similar to the classic rebound affair after a disappointment — it has just about as small a chance of success as love on the bounce, and even more strings attached. In short, adultery can be an act not of love but of timidity, undertaken by a woman who is afraid to resolve her marital problems in case they have no solution but separation and — Oh, horror! — she has to face life on her own without a man.

I am not saying that 'true love' can never exist extra-maritally. Of course it can. I am merely saying that until problems within a woman's marriage have been confronted and a solution or compromise has been found, the quality of her adulterous love will always be ambivalent.

A woman writes, *'I've been married for more than ten years, since I was nineteen. I have an overwhelming physical attraction to a colleague, I think about him, and I know I could fall in love with him. In the past I only once considered being unfaithful (when my husband was drinking heavily) . . .'*

I reply, *'An adulterous affair would merely be a flight from trouble in your marriage. Wouldn't it be a better idea to sort out the mess at home, or put an end to it, before you start messing around outside?'*

In ninety-nine point nine of all problems I come across, my correspondent begins her letter by stating her age: it is the most important and freighted piece of information a woman can give about herself. And thus there is evidence to support my impression that an awful lot of unfaithful women hooked up to their primary men awfully early in life. To take an oath of fidelity at eighteen or nineteen was understandable only when a girl's future was bound to be serial babies and meals on the table. However, to take such an oath or make a serious pledge of exclusivity at eighteen, nineteen, twenty-three, or even older, in this sexy, hopeful, youthful world of ours is perfect folly. Anyhow, these kids were probably madly in love when they undertook to be eternally faithful and their brains, as a result, had all the analytical power of cauliflowers.

Admittedly, I do not like infidelity, which is not to say I think it is 'wrong' or that only 'bad' people go in for it. It's tacky to be in bad faith with someone who trusts you, it's as simple as that. And to be honest, if extra-marital screwing around must be done, I find myself preferring the frankly self-indulgent way men mostly do it. On the whole, it's a shame to see new love dragged in to *excuse* the betrayal of old love.

Yes, there still is a double standard where infidelity is concerned. Male and female infidelity are in different leagues, because, as I've said, women *will* continue to fall in love where they fuck. And sometimes even in this era of contraceptive sophistication, they *will* fall pregnant.

One of the reasons a woman's adultery has always met with greater disapproval than a man's is that men and their families like to be absolutely sure that their heirs and successors are in fact their own flesh and blood. In the days before DNA and blood tests, when he only had her word for it, what greater betrayal could a man imagine than to be foisted off with a baby who was not his own? Even now when disease is the result of illicit sex which worries us most, the possibility of pregnancy still exists and knowing who the daddy is can be a real problem for an unfaithful woman who finds herself in the family way.

A woman writes, *'I'm twenty-six. My husband and I have been trying for a baby for three years. I am pregnant at last, and he is over the moon. The trouble is, I drank too much once after work and had a stupid one night stand. He went back to his homeland where he has a wife and I never want to see him again. But I think my baby could be his. I love my husband body and soul. I regret my infidelity, and I know it would kill him to know about it. We both want this baby so much. What can I do?'*
I reply, *'If I were you, I'd shut up, have the baby, and raise it with the love*

of two good parents — one of whom may or may not be its own by blood. But I am not you. If you undertake this course, do it only, only, only *if you know yourself to be capable of never having your fidelity called into doubt, and of keeping the secret under any circumstances for your entire lifetime. The truth could do terrible mischief to your child if it came out in the future.'*

Never had the wrath of readers fallen more furiously on my head than after this reply was printed! How dared I? A man had a 'right' to know whether the child he raised was his own: he had, in other words, a 'right' to reject it, essentially because of his wife's infidelity. I've thought a lot about that letter, and I am sure that today I'd give the same reply. Here we have a good potential father, and a potentially stable family, and if (*only* if) the mother-to-be knows herself to possess a will of gold, a child will have a good home. So it was not the resident male's dinky sperm that started off the whole miraculous process: what's the big deal? A woman has to know when she gives birth, and how, but paternity has always had some aspects of a movable feast. And a lie of omission (emission?) between a man and woman is perhaps less serious than the destruction of their love and the great loss of a child.

I have a good friend whose well-adjusted, grown-up son has no idea that the father he loves and gets on with well is not actually his own by blood, and the father is equally ignorant of his beloved and only child's true origin: the result of an extra-marital fling his wife had twenty years ago with a Russian artist.

Unfortunately, an agony aunt's advice is delivered in public and lacks the privacy to be found between friends, or between consultant and client, or witch and village lass. The only reservation I have whenever I make an unconventional suggestion is that what I say to one perplexed individual in her special circumstances could be taken as gospel by all those others who are looking for someone to tell them what to think.

Admittedly, a lifetime secret is a melodramatic burden for a woman to carry, but if the circumstances are right, it isn't necessarily unjustified. The trouble is that so many women have such a big appetite for melodrama, there's a real risk that the very idea of a 'lifetime secret' would appeal to the very ones who couldn't keep a secret if their lives depended on it.

On the one hand, imagination must always be brought to bear on the specific case. On the other hand, I wouldn't like my singular advice about uncertain paternity, for instance, to be mistaken as a recommendation for every woman who wants to conceive or is having difficulty in doing so to run right out there and find a sexy donor.

Remembering the furore that broke when I suggested a man be tricked for the sake of a child, by the way, I can't help but wonder how different the public response would have been if men fell pregnant, even a nice fair fifty per cent of the time. But they don't. And conception remains the biggest difference between the sexes, and the most politically fraught.

A woman writes, *'Dear Irma, During a holiday in Kenya I got drunk and slept with one of the safari guides. It meant nothing at the time, but now I'm pregnant. My boyfriend and I have been together for ten years and I know he would be thrilled at the thought of the baby. But we're both white, and the safari guide was black. My boyfriend holds strong religious beliefs about abortion so I don't think he'd tolerate my having one. I'm worried about the AIDS virus, too. I have used my work address because my boyfriend opens all my letters . . .'*

I reply, *'If you share your boyfriend's convictions, then abortion is out of the question for you, and you have no choice: you will have to tell him what occurred and discover whether his religious views tend towards charity and forgiveness — are they humane enough to raise another man's child with love? Once he knows, you two can decide together what to do: adoption, or raise the child.*

'Of course, if you do not share his religious conviction, I imagine it must already be hard to live together, but you have choices. You can arrange an abortion and an HIV test right away, all on your own, put the whole thing behind you, and go on as you were. Then again, if you confess all and he blows up uncharitably, you can leave him and have an abortion, or put the baby up for adoption, or raise it without his help. Can you think of any other alternatives? I can't.

'In your place? I'd confront him. No doubt it would provoke an almighty conflagration, but I'd welcome a showdown with any man who dared to open and read my correspondence . . .'

When a man's sexual appetite starts to flag at home, one of the first suspicions to strike his wife or live-in lover is that it's because there's another woman. In fact, his falling libido is much more likely to be due to lower back pain, ill health or troubles at work. But try telling that to a suspicious mate and see how far you get. Women with reason to know have told me that their unfaithful menfolk actually became *more* attentive at home, sexier, and much nattier and sweeter-smelling than they had ever been before.

'I knew something was up,' a woman I know told me, 'when he suddenly changed his aftershave.'

'That's when you smelt a rat?'

'You bet,' she said. 'He'd never bought his own aftershave in his life. I'd always bought it for him. He wouldn't even know what kind of store to get it. I knew another woman must have chosen it.'

It turned out he'd had a passing affair with an airline hostess (duty-free aftershave), and at the end of some soul-searching (which did their marriage no harm in the long run) my friend forgave him, I'm glad to say. She had a keen nose for trouble. But it's alarming how careless some men can be about their extra-mural entanglements. 'Betrayed's' husband left a letter in his pocket, others have run up bills for two on joint credit cards, left compromising *billets doux* lying around, scattered pocketfuls of unused condoms on the bedroom floor, or sometimes simply spilled the beans one night as they cut into their steak and baked potatoes, after they'd tucked the kiddies up in bed. 'Honey, I'm having an affair,' he says out of the blue, and sets her back on her heels to a degree where she knows things will never, ever be the same.

I really believe that most men are good guys, and if they realised how much pain an infidelity was going to cause the women they lived with, and to what a degree it was bound to damage their primary attachment, they would run a mile from passing love. Certainly they would not leave letters in their pockets, or lipstick on their collars. They'd make damn sure the transgression never came to light. The only possible justifications for confession and the only halfway reasonable excuses for an unfaithful man to leave clues semi-consciously scattered around are all pretty poor, all in all:

1. He knows he has to tell her he's caught an STD.
2. The affair has become serious enough to threaten his primary household.
3. He's not a big enough boy to carry his guilt, and he wants his beloved to punish him, at whatever cost to herself.

4. Provoking a big scene at home can provide a coward with the excuse he may well have been seeking to break it off with an 'Other Woman' who is becoming too demanding, or a bore. 'My wife knows . . .' remain powerful words and have sounded the beginning of the end of countless extra-marital ding-dongs.

The tears and screams of the betrayed woman, her yelling and withholding sex for a while, give him the hard time he thinks he deserves. And, boyishly, the deluded man supposes that after that it will all blow over.

'He cried . . .' says 'Betrayed' and I can hear the awe in her tone. Crying is a highly overrated measure of deep emotions for either sex. Crocodiles cry too, you know. Besides, why should scarcity value make a man's tears any more important than those we women shed too too generously? As often as tears spring from remorse, they are squeezed out by frustration, fear or self-pity. It is bad enough when a woman is blinded by her own tears; to be blinded by *his* tears is going too far into maudlin indulgence. I wish I had a dollar for every time a troubled woman has jumped right back into the frying-pan because 'he cried'!

A woman writes, *'I've been going out with my boyfriend for nearly a year. He constantly tells me he couldn't live without me. I just don't feel the same way — I don't feel "in love" with him. But every time I try to leave, he begs me to stay, and he cries. What can I do?'*
I reply, *'Pass him a box of tissues, and get out while you can . . .'*

Tears shed too often lose their power to persuade, so it's a very short hop from crying to suicide threats, the most wicked weapon of an unhappy man or woman — as far from a measure of love as a guillotine from a butter-knife.

A woman writes, *'He is very dependent and has even threatened suicide if I leave. I am lucky to have a boyfriend who loves me so much, but I feel trapped and, to be honest, I don't know what to do . . .'*
I reply, *'Let me tell you what not to do: never, ever submit to blackmail. If someone puts his life in your hands, hand it back to him. That's not love. That's tyranny. Love makes two stronger together than apart. Your boyfriend is dominating you through his weakness.'*

I know, men are also bullied by the tears of women and their suicide threats, but men don't write to me, or rarely. If they did, I'd tell them precisely the same thing: only the tears of a child deserve to be taken at face value. Of course, if you see your mate as a child and treat her (or him) as an undersized weakling who cannot cope alone, and if she (or he) keeps reinforcing that vision with tears and talk of suicide, then you really are trapped by tyrannical weaknesses, and will stay that way until one of you has the guts to break the evil spell and free two trapped souls.

Whenever an infidelity is revealed, the deceived party is bound to be deeply hurt. The nature of the pain adultery can cause is complex, profound and destructive. I'm not saying that loving unions cannot survive infidelity. On the contrary, sometimes it works as a kind of shock therapy which can correct cracks and flaws that at least one of the original couple had not noticed. But infidelity is a very ugly way to make a lover snap to attention and become more 'perfect'. Also, men generally learn how to use to their advantage the prevalent and appalling feminine failing — the pronounced tendency in some of us to blame ourselves. Boys seem to catch on to this maternal weakness for self-blame about the same time little girls are learning how to manipuate the great male ego. Thus a lot of men, when they are caught out playing around, will desperately accuse their wives or regular girlfriends of all sorts of neglect in order to deflect attention from what is, in truth, their own self-indulgence.

A woman writes, *'Last month my husband owned up to having an affair while I was still breastfeeding our baby, who is now two. I was tired all the time in those days and did not feel like having sex, and he felt very left out. I've told him I understand and I'm sorry. But I just keep thinking about him with another woman and it breaks my heart . . .'*
I reply, *'He was unfaithful, and you apologise? Oh, puh-leeze.'*

Why does infidelity cause pain way, way beyond the sting of sexual jealousy? If there is one word that occurs and recurs in letters to do with infidelity, that word is 'betrayed'. Infidelity is always a betrayal. When you think about it, outside the political arena, big business and the criminal underworld, there are not very many everyday situations in which one person actually has the power to betray another. Granted, every love is special, but love is nevertheless an everyday situation. And love affairs are perfectly set up for betrayal. Because before betrayal can take place some assurance of fidelity has to have been given or understood: a vow, a promise, practically a guarantee. Promises are implicit in pillow-talk. Infidelity is therefore always a betrayal.

Whenever two people love and make love, secrets are shared between them: little ones and big ones, intimate secrets, secrets beyond words, silly secrets, even imagined secrets that only one of them actually knows, though she (or he) would have sworn the other knew them too. When a couple marry or take any firm commitment, they entrust their most secret selves to each other. This is not to say that lovers *should* have no secrets from each other. Give me one good reason to share a secret that accomplishes nothing and causes the loved one nothing but pain. Lies of omission are not always such bad things. Sometimes it is a courtesy not to speak your mind. So what if he doesn't know you keep a journal / don't much like his sister / loved your first boyfriend all those years ago in a special way / sometimes fantasise about Keanu Reeves when making love? Love requires kindness much more than absolute truth — always assuming anybody could know such a thing as absolute truth.

The misery of infidelity comes primarily from the deceived lover's realisation that her secrets and her trust, given in good faith, have been treated with contempt and betrayed to an outsider. Is it rational to feel this way? Not quite. A lot of philandering men try nobly not to mention their wives or steady girlfriends to the 'Other Woman', though it's a pretty sure thing that the Other Woman is doing her best to make him talk. But love is hardly rational in the first place. And besides, nobody is as flustered and scared as women, or men, who have had hope cut out from under them. The betrayal of hope hurts more than any other. And who has been more hopeful than a woman who believed her trust and secrets were safe in love?

Bearing in mind the amalgam of sex with love in the minds of all but a few women, the deceived wife knows, as her man probably does not, that even a two-week affair with his secretary, say, or a fling with a waitress from the diner on the corner, gives the Other Woman (even if only briefly) hope and daydreams that are not rightfully hers.

'Let's not talk about it any more,' says the remorseful husband. 'It was only a passing thing; it meant nothing . . .'

'To you,' thinks his wife, 'but to me it meant a great deal, and to her it meant things you gave me reason to think belonged to me . . .'

A woman writes, *'When I found out he was having an affair, I lost all my self-confidence . . .'*

Another says, *'I thought we were happily married. Then my husband left me for a younger woman. Now, I'm so unsure of myself, I'm even scared to go out shopping or drive the car . . .'*

And, *'I'm nineteen and a student. My boyfriend and I were together for two years. Then he told me there was someone else and he wanted us to break up. I don't want him back. I hate him for hurting me so badly. But I can't concentrate on my work and my grades are suffering . . .'*

The blow to a woman's self-confidence that usually follows her discovery of her man's infidelity is due in part to hurt feelings because he found another more alluring or sexier or nicer to be with than her. But on a level deeper than vanity, she knows herself to have been a sucker, to have been 'had'. A betrayed woman feels a perfect fool, I mean, for having mistaken the guy in the first place and been so sure, so eager, so hopeful, so naive as to have trusted a traitor with her love. Wishful thinking, which once upon a time dressed him in shining armour two sizes too big for him — or for any man — has come home to roost as disappointment.

Each of us is responsible to some degree for her own disappointment, I'm afraid. Much more often than we are deceived by others, or let down by them, we are deceived and let down by our own unjustified or unreal expectations. As a rule, disappointment is an appointment set up by one only, and only for herself. Come the big day, the day of reckoning, the other couldn't make it, or did not even know he was invited, or decided he had better things to do.

It will do no good at all to tell a disappointed woman that she wanted more from Mr Wonderful than she had reason to expect, or more than he was capable of delivering (perhaps she wanted more than was humanly possible), and that's why she is disappointed. She will be in no mood to listen to common sense until the hurt has subsided.

'Where has all the promise gone?' I heard an ageing glamourpuss cry once at the bitter end of her beauty.

'Honey, the only promise worth a damn,' said a man standing nearby, 'is the one you keep.'

'Irma, you get so *pathological*,' an eminent editor once said when I'd been rattling on about the nature of disappointment and the need to replace wishful thinking with understanding. And that isn't all that's pathological about infidelity. Infidelity also contains the grubby little seeds of humiliation. The deceived woman suspects, perhaps with reason, that outsiders must have known what was going on, whispered about it, and called her a 'poor sucker' for still being trustful of a philandering man.

Women like 'Betrayed' will sometimes cry that he used their own bed for his extra-marital sex, as if that made the fact of infidelity worse, which it does, for it means the insensitive brute laid *everything* open to the scorn of a rival, right down to the resident woman's taste in drapes and linen. Even in betrayal there are gentlemanly rules of conduct, and a man who observes them has a far better chance of being forgiven, if and when the time comes for a reckoning.

A man writes, *'How can I evict Mary from my life? She is youth and excitement. Yet, how can I leave my wife, when I know it would destroy her? She knows and likes Mary, we often have dinner together, and she suspects nothing . . .'*

I reply, *'Every hour your wife is permitted to "know and like" a girl she does not realise is her husband's mistress is another hour that will cause her humiliation in retrospect. Perhaps if Mary were older and more compassionate, it is she who would not tolerate such a cruel subterfuge . . .'*

There was a period back in the late sixties when smart big-city couples favoured what they called 'open marriages', which allowed both 'partners', I think is the appropriate word in this case, to play around with other people while remaining 'faithful in spirit' to the marriage. 'Codswallop' was my response back then and I'm afraid time pretty much proved me right. In some cases, one partner played around like a porpoise while the other, not so lucky, stayed home. It used to happen regularly that the playful partner went into a screaming fit when the stay-at-home partner suddenly found a playmate too. And then, eventually, someone would have a baby and confuse the issue no end. More than once, one of the partners actually fell wildly in love with an outsider and went off with him (or her) into a strictly *faithful* old-fashioned union: some of them are still around today, basking in a conventional sunset.

Like it or not, fidelity is a cornerstone of marriage and commitment. Without it, the sexiest couple are simply flatmates in effect. And as long as fidelity matters, infidelity remains a betrayal. What if infidelity doesn't matter to *him*, say, as much as it matters to *her*? (I'm talking here about his own infidelity, of course.) It remains essentially a betrayal, just as long as he *knows* it would matter to her. But how often have we all heard women say that what they don't know can't hurt, and they would rather not know if their mates are playing around? (I have never heard a man say the same thing, regarding the possibility of his wife's infidelity, have you?) A man who is lightheartedly adulterous, and has his wits about him, will be cynical enough, and courteous enough, too, never to let his wife or longterm partner find out about his incidental sport. In our society at least, *she* will probably not see infidelity in the same rosy light as *he* does.

I'm not saying there aren't women as well as men who can be unfaithful, sometimes for the entire length of a marriage, while maintaining a calm front at home, though such a strong will is very, very rare. On the only occasions I've encountered such steadfast infidelity, the woman was not playing around, she was uncompromisingly faithful on two fronts, and the adulterous male partners in the long, long affairs were equally as devoted as she to their primary families and the status quo. These cases, by the way, both involved people much older than my readers and who belonged to a generation that saw itself less belligerently 'entitled' to selfgratification.

Fidelity is an ideal. And the whole point of an ideal is to strive for it, not necessarily ever to achieve it, but to keep on striving for it. An ideal cannot be ruined once and for all because someone fails his promise to live up to it. Ideals are bigger than that: who fails in living up to them, fails himself most of all. Ideals are hard to live up to — that's the point — and thus forgiveness of the genuinely repentant self or the other is all part of achieving them. A reasonable degree of forgiveness must be possible between lovers, it simply has to be, otherwise love itself is called into question, and without love we'd all be in a dreadful pickle.

Fidelity is absolute: he (or she) either is or ain't. It is in their control. (Fantasies and dreams are uncontrollable and don't count. If they did, there could be no fidelity on earth worth speaking of.) But there are degrees of *in*fidelity: the one night stand, the foreign-travel affair, the off-and-on secretary, the long-term mistress, the illicit 'home from home' (sometimes including a child) — all signify very different investments of extra-marital commitment.

Theoretically, infidelity of a lesser degree ought to be relatively easy to forgive. But because it strikes so deep for all those 'pathological' reasons, an infidelity is never as easily forgotten or forgiven as the unfaithful person supposes when he (or she) confesses, or when the affair comes to light.

A woman writes, *'My husband had an affair a year ago and it was eight months before I could let him make love to me again. I still can't bear him touching me . . .'*

Or, *'My boyfriend said it wasn't serious, just one drunken night. I don't want to lose him, but I feel so cheated and hurt. We've agreed not to talk about it any more, but I'm afraid he'll do it again if I don't come to terms with it . . .'*

And, *'Last year my husband owned up to an affair with his secretary. As far as I knew, we had been happy and were planning to start a family. I feel horribly angry with him, as hard as I try not to show it . . .'*

Finally, *'I thought we had a very special marriage. Recently I discovered my husband had had an affair. It only lasted four weeks and he has done his utmost to make it up to me, but I am shattered. I can't discuss it with him, because he has shut it out of his mind . . .'*

The infidelities of men, particularly in middle-age, are not necessarily indications that anything at all is very wrong with their primary households, though I do hold that such is more generally — not always — the case with adulterous *women*. Sometimes his transgression is due to drink, or an aggravated opportunity on a working trip abroad, say, or a drooping ego that needs a boost; or he's taken unawares by the predatory behaviour of a young stranger, or he wonders if he can still cut the mustard, or the other guys dare him — the list is endless and the reasons are nowhere near as serious as love.

Even when the infidelity was not due to any problem in a man's marriage in the first place, it could well become a problem in his marriage once the cat is out of the bag. Unless his wife is as wise as

Solomon, and probably as old, she is going to assume it *was* the marriage and something 'wrong' with her that set him prowling in alleys new. And whatever he had hoped would happen when the truth came out, his infidelity will not be seen as nothing more serious than a parking violation in the eyes of his resident woman: it will require a lot of time, masses of affection, much talk, talk, talk, and tons of reassurance if confidence in herself and trust in him is to be restored in her heart of hearts.

Let him imagine that one almighty explosion has cleared the air and everything can go back to normal: 'I'm sorry. I love you. Now, let's say no more about it . . .' And perhaps she won't say any more about it, not to him: she'll write to me, or cry into her pillow, and pretend even to herself that she has forgiven him. So why, oh why, does remembering hurt so much? And why is she so afraid that he will do it again?

The accidental adulterer's best bet, it seems to me, is to keep his (or her) big trap shut and to try not to let it happen again. Not an ideal solution, to be sure, but given what we require of love, infidelity is hardly an ideal condition.

• • • • • • • • • •

Dear 'Betrayed',

You say you thought you were a happily married woman. You were a happily married woman. And you will be again. You say you have forgiven your husband. But you haven't. It is no good pretending to him or yourself that the business is over and done with. In your mind, it isn't. Not yet. Some betrayed women feel angry, others like you feel hurt — either way, the man has a mile or two to go yet before he can be forgiven.

You say you have agreed not to mention what happened. Is that a mutual agreement? Or did his tears persuade you to let up on him before you really felt quite agreeable to forget, and forgive? Tell him as calmly as you can that you need to say more and know more about what happened, and why it happened, and how he intends never to let it happen again. Explain that it is still disturbing you and, as much as you want to let go of it, you need more help from him before you can. Let him know exactly how you feel so he can comfort you this time and dry your tears.

If he does not understand and is not willing to talk out an experience which is not over and will not be until you say so, it seems to me you will have to take a very strong stand: until he helps you get over your hurt the marriage is non-existent. If needs be, tell him you want marital counselling. Remember, he broke faith with you, you have nothing to be ashamed about.

Once it is all out in the open — the hurt, explanation and apology, and in due course the start of real forgiveness — I'm sure his genuine love for you and his steady fidelity will allow the incident to slip much deeper into the healing past and make your memory of it much more bearable, much sooner than you can imagine now. Things won't be the same, they never are, but they will be as good. And what your marriage has lost in gloss, it may well make up for in truth and understanding.

Yours faithfully,

Aunt Irma

● ● ● ● ● ● ● ● ● ●

AGONY AUNT'S WORKSHEET

1. In order to make a life together, do two people need to hold the same ideals?
2. Is it possible to love more than one sexual partner at the same time?
3. If you make love to a man you love are you betraying the other man you promised to love?
4. If the man who promised to love you makes love to another woman he loves, is he betraying you?
5. In your opinion, and why, is a man's infidelity less serious / more serious / as serious as a woman's?
6. One good reason, please, to confess an infidelity that is over and done. And four good reasons not to.
7. Write your own reply to 'Betrayed'.

PROBLEM SEVEN

Is there life after loneliness?

• • • • • • • • • •

Dear Irma,

I am twenty-five. I've been living with my boyfriend for four years and we are stuck in a rut. I'm bored. We seem to be together out of habit more than anything else. Even our sex life is routine: either he's too tired, I'm too tired, or we just do it like a duty. I fantasise about life as a single again. But everyone I know is part of a couple. If we split up my evenings would be empty. Whenever I think I'm going to end it, I feel panicky. I feel I'm missing out on a lot, but at the same time I can't face life without him. How would I cope with the inevitable loneliness?

'Scared'

• • • • • • • • • •

'Don't you find,' I was once asked by a friend (a psychiatrist, it so happens), 'that loneliness is *always* the problem . . .?' Yes and no. Rarely do I receive letters like this one from 'Scared' that actually mention the word 'loneliness' — perhaps one out of every thousand. Even more rarely, however, is loneliness, or fear of loneliness, *not* to be found at the very core of the problem, or someplace near it.

I've often heard it said (mostly by men) that if the women who wrote to me were not lonely why wouldn't they have a friend, a sister, a mother, *someone* closer to consult in their agony than a snapshot at the top of a page in a glossy magazine? An agony aunt is anybody's. And sometimes, especially when the writer is very young, it is true that she writes to me because there is quite simply nobody else she dares tell when she is pregnant, say, or addicted, homosexual or suicidal. Frequently, the mother or teacher in a position to be honoured by a girl's confidence is so full of *shoulds* and prejudices, they scare her away. Anyhow, what's the point of asking for help from someone whose reply will be as predictable as a party political broadcast? And sometimes, of course, thoughtlessly judgemental or brutal parents are the problem themselves.

For the most part, however, it isn't loneliness that drives women to consult a stranger like me. Troubled women as often as not are surrounded by colleagues, friends and family. But friends and relatives play assigned roles when a woman is in emotional turmoil: they listen, listen, and listen again to her; they repeat what they said last time without much hope of being heard; they give advice which is misinterpreted and even ignored, unless it's what she *wants* to hear, in which case a fat lot of good it will do her.

Furthermore, to write the problem down and send it to an agony aunt means she has to stand back from her pain. Writing hard words on paper is but a small first step, but a step nevertheless, towards understanding. So when I say that loneliness is often near the centre of the troubles I come across, I do not mean to suggest that the troubled girl must lack friends or why would she write to me? On the contrary, sometimes a sympathetic stranger is a better bet for consolation than someone close and deeply concerned. An outsider's point of view works like an anchor on a storm-driven boat: it pulls her up short, at least for a moment, and lets her catch her breath.

And now we're on the topic, believe me, I am in no circumstance nominating myself as someone who 'is there for her', as in:

'My father was never there for me . . .'
'My mother wanted a boy and she was never there for me . . .'
'My boyfriend says he loves me, so why isn't he there for me . . .?'
'He still goes out every weekend with his friends. He should be there for me, but I don't feel like he is . . .'

Nobody is 'there for you', nobody *should* be 'there for you', and nobody *can* be 'there for you'. The people who are important in your life are there for you to love as well as you can; they love you back if they are able, as much as they are able. They help you when they can, as much as they can and are willing to help you; you help them, don't you? As much as you can and are willing to. But let's get something straight once and for all: they are not there for you.

The suckers in this world are those who believe they are entitled to be repaid for what they give: not what they sell, mind you, or barter by agreement, but what they *give*. Our strength does not reside in what we get from life and others, but entirely in what we give to it and to them. And if that doesn't make sense to you yet, come back again when you're grown up.

A young woman writes, *'I'm seventeen but very mature for my age. I want to have a baby so there will always be somebody there for me . . .'*
I reply, *'Is that why your mother had you? And are you there for her? Somehow, I doubt it. Please try to wait until you know you are ready to give a new life the chance to be there for its own sweet self . . .'*

'Being there for me . . .' reflects a spiritual laziness, another so-called 'right' with no expenditure of energy or self. It is a vain, uncharitable little concept, pumped up with ego, generally said in a whining tone, used in blame or accusation, and another cliché I would like never to see or hear again, especially when the subject is love. 'Being there for me' belongs in the nursery, and I am appalled to hear women use it, which they do, it seems to me, much more often than men. As a woman stumbles out into freedom at last, what hope is there for her maturity and achievement if she is persuaded of her 'right' to have someone there who will hold her hand? If ever there was a notion designed to increase loneliness and alienation in our society it has got to be the very idea that someone, anyone, has a duty to be there because you want them to be there for *you*.

Let's leave it like this: people are there, that's all. And when you love someone, you're grateful to your luck that he is there. But he is there for himself, to be himself and give of himself as well as he can, just as you are here for yourself, to be yourself and give of yourself — your understanding, your humour, your personality — as well as you can. I'm glad to get that off my chest. Because I think loneliness is a profound and serious part of modern life that doesn't have much to do with whether or not someone is 'there for you'.

My psychiatrist friend maintains that loneliness results from the severing of the umbilical cord. He makes loneliness sound downright wholesome. Market researchers have found that poor people are lonelier than the prosperous, the old feel lonelier than the young, and housewives feel three per cent lonelier than working spinsters. Are married men, I wonder, less lonely than playboys? Is the prison guard more or less lonely than the prisoner? Are you lonelier than me, and are we both lonelier than an astronaut on his way to the moon, or an Australian Aborigine on solitary walkabout? Statistics may be helpful for selling soap and soup, but loneliness is a feeling, and like all feelings it is subjective and impossible to measure or compare.

Even though when most boys and girls tell an agony aunt they are 'lonely' they actually mean to say they want sex, I do not believe that the absence of lovers, any more than the absence of sympathetic friends and family, is what causes loneliness.

A woman writes, *'I'm desperately lonely. I have so much to give and nobody to share it with me.*
I reply, *'If sharing what we have could really end our loneliness, then how could there be so many lonely mothers, and lonely fathers, and lonely flatmates, and lonely people in the crowd?'*

Sorry, 'Scared', here I go, getting 'pathological' again, when all I want to say is this: nobody is alone in being lonely around here. Loneliness is built into the way we live. And the key to our loneliness, I think, is not lack (of companions or lovers) but loss: loss of nature, loss of faith, loss of purpose, loss of giving a damn about each other — and ultimately, the very essence of loneliness, loss of self.

A woman writes, *'I'm normally a cheerful, outgoing person, but lately I have been obsessed by thoughts of death, my own death and the death of my* *boyfriend, my mother, everyone. I lie awake at night, thinking about death . . .'*

Another woman writes, *'I can't stop thinking about the possibility of a Third World War . . .'*

Still another writes, *'There's so much pain and poverty in the world. I want to do more to help . . .'*

See? Not *all* the letters that come my way are from young women troubled by men. Only about ninety-five per cent. Once in a while someone writes under the pressure of a troubling feeling that has come from outside her own self-centred emotional concerns. And generally her distress, understandable and perfectly natural, is thanks to a glimpse of what our common loneliness is all about.

Being alone does not mean being lonely. Loneliness is not imposed on us from outside, it is the space within where once there was some-thing or where maybe someday there will be something. Nobody can 'cure' a space; the best we can do is begin to fill it. How we choose to fill it is an expression of ourselves and our personalities; it takes some learning, some experience, and it is worth taking time. People in haste to fill up with something they hope will end their loneliness are the ones who follow cult leaders into cataclysms, and the girls who write to me pregnant at sixteen, and the women who throw their youth away on shabby or hopeless romances because they want 'someone there for them' and have neither the patience nor the cour-age to sit all alone for a while and simply be there.

But just because I fancy myself a cut-rate existentialist does not mean that 'Scared' has written to me for some cut-rate existential philosophy. All I need to say is that the 'inevitable loneliness' she fears when she leaves her very bad union will not be the result of being alone; in fact it will not be loneliness at all. How could she be more lonely than she has been these past years, locked into a small space with a man whose company she no longer wants or enjoys?

'Scared' is already as alone as a woman can be, so are the others like her who stay in dreary or brutal relationships because they fear the alternative which they call 'loneliness'. But it isn't loneliness they are afraid of. How can it be? They are all lonely people already.

'Scared' and the others are afraid of independence, afraid to ex-plore, afraid to discover; they are afraid of the freedom to act on nobody's say-so but their own; they are afraid of the risk of making mistakes. And I guess they are afraid of their own company.

I wish I could advise every woman who is unhappy with a lover or husband to get herself out immediately, as she could very well find herself a lot less lonely when she is alone. I can't, however, because responsibilities count for as much in this life — and more — than rights: we claim our rights now, our responsibilities live on into the future. And as much as I love a general rule, many women find themselves responsible for more than just themselves and their own happiness: they have children.

A woman writes, *'My boyfriend and I have a two-year-old daughter, but he treats me like dirt, and I wonder why I stay with him . . .'*

Admittedly, when a couple has children to consider, splitting up is a complex business. And under some circumstances, if both parents are deeply attached to their children and involved with them, there are good reasons for staying together. The mutual love a couple feel for their children can be strong enough to nourish a family and sustain it, after the grown-ups no longer feel passion for each other.

However, when an unhappy woman stays with a man who insults her, beats her, humiliates her and generally 'treats her like dirt', the damage to their children must be taken into account. What the kids will see as an acceptable degree of debasement (or why would mama accept it?) can distort the way they love later, when they're grown up, and can certainly make the break-up of the household a very good idea.

When it comes to staying together for the children, there is no black-and-white rule, and nothing is perfect. Otherwise, as long as a woman is childless, of all the reasons she thinks she needs to stay with a man who bores her, or disgusts her, or 'treats her like dirt', the least worthy is because she is afraid to be on her own . . . No, hang on! Wait a minute! I feel a prejudice coming on. Yes. There is one excuse and only one for clinging to a bad home-life that I like even less than fear of loneliness.

A woman writes, *'We have no real contact any more. There's nothing much between us. He doesn't even notice that sex with him turns me off, and we never talk. I want to leave. But we have a lovely house, I have my own car, and I'd never be able to afford this lifestyle on my own . . .'*

I reply, *'If the sex turns you off, what are you doing it for? Money, I guess. And there's a name for that . . .'*

It's easy for me to say, I know. I am fully employed at the moment and, come the crunch, there is always waiting on tables. Next to writing, waitressing was my favourite of the many jobs I've held; I was good at it, and I could do it again at a pinch. Since childhood, nobody has ever supported me financially. I don't know why I'm so proud of that fact, I'm sure it's a weakness in my character. But what the hell, nobody's perfect.

Heaven knows I've been broke for most of my life, and sometimes desperate for the rent money. But to love, or pretend to love, or even just commit an act of love for money? I won't call it 'wrong' — the flesh-peddling business has been around for long enough to have achieved a kind of venerability, specious though it is. However, I have to say that the idea of selling bodies, even to those in desperate need of them, really goes against my grain. Prostitutes are not bad people; I've known a few who were amusing company. And I can even acknowledge that their profession is useful in a way, to about the same degree as a whistle on a kettle. However, on the three or four occasions girls have written to me to justify prostitution as a way of paying off their debts or in one case to pay for a college degree, I've given them a sharp piece of my mind and recommended waitressing as a cleaner, safer and in the long run much less alienating and lonely-making alternative. I cannot admire screwing for money; I find it squalid and soul-destroying, and besides, the hire does not equal the risks.

The loneliness 'Scared' and others like her say they fear so much that it keeps them stuck with men they no longer love or like has many components and, I'll grant you, one of them can be financial insecurity if they kiss his pay packet goodbye. Being broke alone is a whole lot more scary than being broke in company. Nevertheless, I'm glad to say not much evidence comes my way that money is often uppermost in an unhappy woman's mind. Materialism hardens hearts and makes people pretend emotions they cannot actually feel: the flip side of fake sentimentality is always cruelty. Creature comfort has its place in love, but fear of discomfort is a crummy excuse for cowardice.

And then there is shame. Good old shame. Where would we be

without it? Happier, I dare say, and kinder to each other. Our society, it seems to me, can even now feel like a pretty shameful place in which to be a woman on her own.

Shame is a lonesome feeling which, paradoxically I guess, depends upon other people. We feel shame before others and what we think they are thinking. And we feel shame when we imagine how we would look if others could see what we were up to. 'Aren't you ashamed of yourself?' a mother asks her little girl, and the child hangs her head, ashamed of what she was doing, yes, but only because she was caught doing it.

A woman writes, *'How can I stop blushing whenever I meet a man?'*

Another says, *'I freeze whenever I have to talk to strangers . . .'*

And, *'I want to go to Weight Watchers but I'm too scared of what people will think . . .'*

It's a very fine line between public shyness and private shame. Adolescence is the time when the two feelings most frequently overlap and there is something perpetually adolescent about any woman (or man) who worries, sometimes to the point of paralysis, about how she appears to others, and who suffers intense private shame which nine times out of ten she calls 'loneliness'.

Funny, isn't it, in the old days shame fell on girls who went out and did 'it', now it falls on the girl who stays at home alone and doesn't.

'Everyone I know is part of a couple,' writes 'Scared', explaining her reluctance to get out of a dead-end affair, her fear of 'inevitable loneliness'. A woman on her own can find herself thinking that others must believe she isn't worth very much, or why wouldn't a man have claimed her company? Then, in a short time a woman on her own can find herself starting to think as she believes other do: she can't be of much value, or why doesn't a man move in on her?

A woman writes, *'I'm twenty-two. My friends say I'm pretty and I dress well. But I haven't even had a date in more than a year. More and more of my friends are in couples. I'm tired of crying all alone at night. What's wrong with me?'*

I reply, *'You're young, you're pretty, you dress well, and you have friends.*

Nothing is wrong with you. Bear in mind all that is right with you and let people see it.'

Of course the shame of manlessness, or 'loneliness', as manless women (and womenless men) are mistakenly heard to call it, carries a sexual burden like an awful lot of human shame. What do people on their own do for sex? Presumably, the best they can.

Masturbation is sometimes called the 'lonely vice', though in fact it is more solitary than lonely, and it is hardly a vice at all. A lot of the mostly young women who write to me are worried about masturbating because it seems to imply a confession that no partner has volunteered or been seduced into the livelier game.

A woman writes, *'Because I have no sex life, I masturbate three or four times a week. Whenever I do it, I feel so sad and lonely afterwards . . .'*
I reply, *'If you feel sad and lonely afterwards and you felt sad and lonely before, then at least while you're doing it, it relieves you of feeling sad and lonely. And what is wrong with that?'*

True enough, in a society devoted to group activities the way ours is, and to coupledom, being on one's own can easily look like failure. But surely common sense alone is enough to show us there is no reason for shame. On the contrary, there is great reason for pride when you spend some considerable time independent of the prevailing style of thinking.

There is only one person I can imagine as lonely as the woman in an unhappy love affair or marriage and that's the one who goes along with what her crowd says because she's afraid to think for herself.

A woman writes, *'I'm twenty-one and still a virgin. I want to wait for someone special. But I'm the only virgin I know, and my friends make me feel like a freak . . .'*
I reply, *'You have taste, principles, romance and self-control. Any bunch of people who make you feel like a "freak" for these qualities are not friends, and not worth worrying about . . .'*

There is only one treatment for shame and that is to stop feeling it. How do you stop feeling it? You unglue your opinions from those of the people around you. You think for yourself, in other words, and then you look the rest of the world straight in the eye, knowing that you know better than anyone what holds true for you. Is it lonely to think alone? Not in the least. It is losing yourself in the common way of thinking *without* thinking for yourself that causes loneliness. It is losing yourself in sex, in drugs, in pointless noise, that makes loneliness. Loneliness is losing yourself.

When you think for yourself, then you have to see, for example — and not because I say so — that there is absolutely nothing 'wrong' with a woman (or man) staying in alone on Saturday night, or living alone, or travelling alone, or choosing her own company, or staying a virgin until she freely chooses to let someone deserving share all she has to offer.

Given how quickly young women jump to conclusions, I'd better make it clear I am not advocating virginity for one and all. Virgins can be as lonely as whores, especially if their virginity is imposed on them and not a choice they've made for themselves. There's a ton and a half of loneliness to be found in obeying rules that have no relevance and make no sense to you.

A woman writes, *'My relationship with my boyfriend has been going from bad to worse in the four years since we've been living together. When I do something he doesn't like, sometimes he won't speak to me for days. I'm twenty-two and he's four years older. There's this guy I've been seeing at work who is kind, goodlooking, and everything I've ever wanted. He says he loves me and wants to live with me. Can I trust him?'*
I reply, *'Never mind trusting him. You have been living with a dominating lover since you were a girl of eighteen. What makes you think you can trust yourself . . .?'*

I remember once hearing a film star who was marrying for the fourth or fifth time say to an audience of millions, 'This is the real thing. I'll never be lonely again. I've found myself at last!' If it really was herself she'd been looking for over the years, then she must have been looking in some odd places. And if it was herself she thought she'd found at last in the man beside her, then she wasn't seeing very clearly: he was fifteen years younger than she, considerably prettier, taller, and besides he was a man. Judging from the intoxicated fire in his eyes, the only thing he and she had in common was a massive self-importance.

We all do most of our growing up when we're alone, and any woman who flits from one man to another with no solitary time in between will quite simply never grow up. When a woman leaves her stale affair or marriage for another man, she will be bound to take half her problems along. Time between men, solitary time, though it may not be fun-filled, will show you more of who you are and who you want to be than your reflection in the lovesick eyes of the next man.

'If we split up,' says 'Scared', 'my evenings would be empty . . .' In the preceding line she complained of 'boredom' with her lover. Presumably, he bores her. But if she is equally scared of being bored without him, what is left for me to think except that she bores herself too? If she is bored in her own company, it is really very unlikely she will ever find herself other than bored in anyone else's company. Unless she goes to live with a stand-up comic. And even that would probably get boring when she'd heard his routines for the tenth or twelfth time.

Half of being bored in a marriage or a love affair, half of being bored in general, is being boring, I'm afraid. And most of being boring is the result of having developed no resources to fall back on in solitude or to share in company. That's why kids are so easily and often bored, and so boring about it when they are. Resources take time to cultivate and they are cultivated almost exclusively in time alone when there is nobody around to relieve you of the need to entertain yourself.

What sort of entertainment needs no company? For a start, there's thinking. Thinking is a perfectly wholesome solitary activity. Fair enough, nobody sits around all day thinking, or thinks she does. Nevertheless, nobody can think much at all who has not spent time thinking for herself and by herself. The best way to solve a problem is to pull back from it to a point where it can be seen whole, from more than one side, and from that vantage point a workable solution will often gradually appear. People often ask if reading daily letters from troubled people doesn't bore me to tears. No agony letter has *ever* bored me, every one of them starts me weighing and analysing, imagining and remembering, and choosing my words — *thinking*, in effect. Thought and boredom are incompatible.

'Oh, I never think,' a woman I know said to me, and she sounded proud of herself, too. 'I feel my way to all my decisions.' Undoubtedly one of the silliest things I've ever heard. She thinks for sure — we all do, we have to — she just doesn't think she thinks, and obviously she doesn't think more than she has to. The decisions she proudly claims to have felt her way to include two failed marriages, an on-again, off-again love affair with another woman's husband, and countless attempts to find a congenial way to pay her bills. Could she have done any worse by trying to feel a little less and think more? I doubt it.

Are there still girls so out-of-date they don't want other people, especially men, to think they think? Thinking remains a very underrated activity, especially among women, many of whom see it as somehow unfeminine and less attractive, more butch and wrinkle-making, than feeling. I'm not knocking feeling, mind you. Only next time you're alone on Saturday night and feeling bored, before you say you're 'lonely', think about what you are feeling. Don't rush out anywhere with anyone as if your house were haunted and you had to get away from it, because *that* really is boring and, what's more, spending time with people simply in order not to be alone is asking for real one-hundred-per-cent loneliness in the long run.

People who *need* people are the unluckiest people in the world. People who need to be needed by people are almost as unlucky. Liking the people whose company you choose is good, however, and worth waiting for.

I'm not all that much of a social crusader, probably because problems come my way one at a time. However, there is one bandwagon I ride with pride, all the more because there's nobody on it but me. It is my very own Going Out Alone Society — GOAS. Membership: one. Tell me why any solitary person should sit at home, unrung, unloved, unchosen, and full of shame? Cities such as ours, in which many people live alone, are also the first to allow a single woman into practically any entertainment unescorted without anyone noticing or giving much of a damn. During the last century, perhaps a girl all by herself in a public place would have been looked at disapprovingly or dangerously. But now that we are able to pay our own way, whose business is it if we choose to go wherever we please? Here we have a genuine, one-hundred per cent guaranteed right. Can anyone tell me where the law is found that says theatres, concerts, cinemas, parks, holidays, restaurants and other entertainments are closed to a woman (or a man) on her own?

'Oh, I couldn't!' a young friend of mine cried when I suggested she go to a movie she wanted to see by herself instead of waiting hopelessly for someone to invite her. 'I'd be scared,' she said vaguely.

'Of what?'

'I don't know . . .' she said, looking troubled.

If she is afraid of being attacked by a savage rapist, then surely she is as safe in a crowd as sitting alone in her room. If, on the other hand, my friend and girls like her are afraid of being seen to be alone, then that is merely good old shame again, and an unworthy excuse to keep her from a movie or any other event. A good movie holds as much interest and entertainment for a single person as for a couple. In any case, most strangers are much too interested in themselves, believe me, even to notice the woman in their midst all on her own. People who do notice the Lone Ranger or pay the slightest attention to her will see her precisely as she presents herself: not embarrassed, not if she's a member of my society, only bright and eager for her share of pleasures open to anyone with the price of admission.

There are Native American tribes that send their youngsters out for a time to live by themselves in the wilderness as part of their initiation into adulthood. It is important that they should master the tools of survival needed on long hunting trails, but it is also important that each young person should come to terms with his own thoughts and his own personality (and his own nightmares) in order that he can work alone and sustain himself. Only a person able to survive alone is considered ready to work in harmony within adult society.

The wilderness in *our* lives is of a different variety. I can't ship every girl and boy out there to grow up the only way it's possible to do so, alone. I only wish that to each woman stuck in a miserable household, and each girl rushing into marriage because she's scared of being left all by herself on the shelf, I could send a single ticket to the movie of her choice — that's all, just a movie — on the condition she go to it by herself and perhaps for the first time in her life find she can actually survive doing a little something without company.

For whatever reason any girl is scared to be and to do and to go on her own (and this goes for 'Scared' too), getting over it on her own will be the beginning of the end of loneliness. Every happy life is led with an element of what-the-hell. And a little anarchy in the soul of a single woman helps to upset conventions and allay prejudice, including her own, if she encounters it out in the big world.

Is independence a selfish condition? I don't think it is. It's the dependent person who only sees others as 'being there for her' (who in other words does not see others as being at all apart from her own needs) who is the self-centred one. She is bound to be disappointed and will almost certainly complain of loneliness one day. And it is she, by the way, who will rush into commitment to a man who is probably as scared in his own way as she, and she who will call herself 'mature' when in fact the lonely space within her is as empty as it was the day she was born.

By now it has certainly become clear, at least it has to me, that I think true loneliness has very little to do with a lack of companions, and everything to do with an inability to be alone. Shortage of friends and lovers may be an itch, but it's failure to be content in your own company that is a flaming pain.

Solitude and loneliness are only the same for a woman who has developed no skills of independence and who is still waiting like a baby to be given by someone else (a man) what she can perfectly well find alone and cultivate for sharing: interests, experiences and areas of happiness. All the clubs, parties, friends, lovers and agony aunts cannot make a woman one whit less afraid of loneliness if she is unwilling ever to be alone.

• • • • • • • • • •

Dear 'Scared',

How can a man with whom you have no real pleasures in common stand between you and 'inevitable loneliness'? What do you imagine loneliness to be if not the isolation and emptiness you are feeling now within your love affair? You're not afraid of loneliness, you are afraid of being alone, which is not the same thing; you are afraid of standing on your own two feet with no man to give you identity as half a couple. You are, in other words, afraid of growing up.

Grown-ups are never bored, their trouble generally is finding time in the day to do all they want to do or are required to do. Who knows, perhaps if you were more grown-up and self-sufficient your love affair would not have drifted into these shallows. But that is by the by. What you must do for yourself now is see to it that you never again find yourself in a stagnant backwater because you are afraid of loneliness.

You have three choices: stay as you are, wait around for another man to rescue you from this one (and then another man to rescue you from that one, and so on), or get out and find out who you are when you are by yourself — who you are, in other words. It isn't easy and it isn't all fun to face the world on your own, but after a while you'll start to enjoy it, and in the end when you do meet someone you want to live with, you'll be a whole person with lots and lots to share, so the word 'boredom' need never cross your mind again.

You say you are together with your boyfriend out of no more than habit. Sometimes, the best way to break a habit is cold turkey. As an exercise, I recommend you go away to a city or town where you've never been before; check in all alone to a motel for a few days. Take a Walkman, your favourite music, a notebook and pen, maybe something to read, settle in, and sweat it out.

When two or three days in solitude are done, and a few meals taken alone in public, you may find you have begun to discover things about yourself and your capabilities that you never knew before.

Bon Voyage,
Aunt Irma

● ● ● ● ● ● ● ● ● ●

AGONY AUNT'S WORKSHEET

1. When you are all on your own, name what it is exactly you are afraid of.
2. List as many chores and activities as you can that you need to be on your own to do.
3. Why do you consider yourself good company?
4. Which would you rather have on Saturday night: a blind date, the wrong date, or no date? Give three reasons why.
5. Name six items you would take to a desert island, least important first.
6. Write your own answer to 'Scared'.

PROBLEM EIGHT

What are friends for?

• • • • • • • • • •

Dear Irma,

Last week at a club I saw my best friend's boyfriend with another girl. I wasn't going to jump to any conclusions, but then I saw him kiss her. I was furious. My friend is crazy about this boy. They've been together for two years and are talking about marriage. I want to tell her what I saw, but I am afraid she won't believe me. I've never liked her boyfriend and made no secret of my feelings. I don't want to spoil my friendship with her, but if I don't tell her what I saw, how can I look her in the eye again?

'Torn'

• • • • • • • • • •

It looks so simple at first reading, but if it were that simple, then 'Torn' wouldn't be torn, would she?

When you see a friend's boyfriend kissing another girl, do you tell her? Not always. Friendship puts other considerations ahead of truth — assuming, that is, that you know the truth. The only time I ever saw a friend's lover embracing another girl, I went to a party that night and was introduced to the girl I'd seen him with: it was his sister. Admittedly, when a man kisses a girl in a public place, the girl is not usually a close relative, but at the same time, what you are seeing could be not what it appears, or a lot less than it appears. If you must tell anyone what you have seen, and you are in a position to do so, then *he* is the one who needs to know, as it is up to him to explain and to clean up his act.

Friendship is complicated. Love affairs are essentially a lot more simple than friendships for the very reason that sex is involved. Physical attraction pulls lovers to each other and glues them together, for a while at least, until habit, shared joys and troubles, babies, houses and in-laws cement the deal. Then, if the lovers are very, very lucky, and kind to each other, and relatively selfless, they may find they are also truly each other's friends. Yet it is a lot more unusual than the women who write to me believe that a pair of lovers remain real friends after the sexual spell is broken. Only when they have genuinely been friends to start with, when they have hurt no feelings and played no games — it is rare, but it can happen — can they drift away from each other physically without hard feelings on either side, and no lingering passion to muck up their friendship.

A woman writes, *'Our relationship is over. But I want us to be friends . . .'*

Another writes, *'We have agreed to start seeing other people but to stay friends . . .'*

Or, *'How do I make him see I just want us to stay friends?'*

Alarm bells ring whenever I read the phrase, 'I want us to be just friends . . .', for it means, first of all, that the writer doesn't believe a friend's love ranks up there with romantic love, or why her 'just'? And second, I do not trust the coolness of her heart. Friendship between ex-lovers requires, first of all, that neither one of them should have been hurt deeply by the break-up. Hurting people is downright unfriendly. And when you have been hurt, you do not forgive, or forget, as quickly as you would like to, or believe you *should*. Any woman who has been dumped by a man or is in pain at the end of a love affair, when she tells me she 'just wants them to be friends', makes me suspect she is still hooked, and hoping he will relent and love her again.

I am not precisely saying she still loves him, by the way. It is simply that when a love affair ends badly it leaves the rejected lover with a mystery. That's why bad men are harder to forget than sweethearts: because they remain a puzzle unsolved and therefore obsessional. 'If only . . .', the dumped woman thinks over and over again, especially late at night when she'd be better off asleep. 'If only I had done "X", or said "Y" . . .'

A woman writes, *'We were together for four years. Last year he told me he didn't love me and there was someone else. I see them together sometimes, he is very cold to me, and it hurts so much. I know it's finished between us. I only want us to be friends . . .'*

I reply, *'He dumped you. He went off with someone else. He's said he doesn't love you. He's cold when you meet. And you say you "only want to be friends"? Who are you kidding? The truth is, you want things back the way they can never be again. He has hurt you and he does not deserve your friendship. Do your best to dislike him intensely, until the day comes (it will come) when thinking of him no longer matters. Then, be friends if that is what you still want. But you won't want it . . .'*

'I just want us to be friends . . .' really means she wants to go back and unravel the mystery of why love ended so badly. She's blaming herself, in other words, and longs to put things right again. It is a version of regret, backwards-looking and not very realistic. Because she and he aren't friends, they weren't friends in the first place: they were 'just' lovers.

A woman writes, *'There is this guy at work and we are really good friends, but I want something more . . .'*

And, *'Sometimes I catch him looking at me in a way that makes me wonder if we could be more than friends . . .'*

And again, *'He's a good friend. We talk about everything. But I want more. Only I'm afraid to lose his friendship . . .'*

These women may call them 'friends', but obviously these fellows don't share their deepest, practically uncensored thoughts the way good friends do (something else friends are for). If they did, then to blazes with flirting — friends don't flirt with each other — any of these women could tell the man in question straight out she wanted his body, and if they were really on a friendly wavelength, he would have guessed it already. Should he reply, 'Thanks, but I'd really rather not,' there would be no harm done, they'd go out for a beer or a coffee, and the friendship would continue.

To be honest, when a woman has a true man-friend, he is likely to be a brotherly figure with whom she has probably never had sex, for whatever reason, and probably never wanted it. When you find a friendly man unbearably sexy, you are *not* good friends, in fact, or any kind of friends at all. You are a member of the opposite sex, wondering whether or not to try getting it on with him. Flirtation is a game with but one goal, and that ain't friendship. Early flirtation is a gossamer thing, based on glances and flutters, and not much more than a hint of desire. In the past, women were brave about initiating the game, but letters from frightened flirts have been steadily increasing in recent years. Have girls in the wake of liberation become ashamed of old skills? Of the ability to plant an idea, for example, without aggression or commitment?

Certainly in our private lives, and I think probably in our professional lives too, there is a growing danger of our using what we have earned in terms of equality to behave self-importantly, pompously, defensively: some of us appear to have liberated the weak men within us, rather than the strong women. For instance, have we forgotten the fun of baiting, angling, hooking — flirting? If we have, then we really are taking ourselves awfully, horribly, *male*-ishly seriously.

When anyone of either sex makes a flirtatious overture, to be turned down is always a threat, and don't kid yourself that he is not as scared of rejection as you, or as easily hurt by it. Could be he is gay, or otherwise engaged, but there is at least an equal chance, especially if he's young, that your fanciable friend is just as frightened as you of being rejected.

And yes, it could be he simply does not fancy you as anything sexier than a platonic friend. But if you are afraid to take the risk, and he won't make a move, then you will never know and must remain locked in stalemate. Proceed cautiously, think not of what you want, but be sensitive to what he is telling you, and leave plenty of time for him to respond. Then if he turns out to be too hard a nut to crack, only your hopes will be dashed (they were badly placed to begin with). As long as you can walk away with a smile on your face, even if it trembles a little, no great harm need be done to your pride or your friendship.

When a girl wants 'more than friendship' with a friend, she is correct to worry that sex could come between them and leave her with neither friend nor lover. Sexual attraction is in many ways the antithesis of friendship. Friends can be with each other comfortably, even at their most vulnerable. Freedom to seek each other out when they are at their lowest and plainest is one of the things friends are for. But two people who fancy each other flirt, and flirtation is tense and coy, showing only the side that stirs and inflames lust. Lust is a blunt and insensitive feeling, it knows what it wants, but not much else; it sees what it wants, but not half of what it is bargaining for.

A woman writes, *'My husband has just informed me he's handed in his notice and is going into business. We have to sell our house and move into cheaper property and I will have to give up the job I love and go into something that pays better. How on earth am I going to live with all this? Not that my husband isn't a sensitive person; apart from all else, he's my best friend . . .'*

I reply, *'You mean your "best friend" has sold the ground out from under you? That doesn't sound very friendly to me. And it seems a little odd that you have chosen to confide in me, a stranger, instead of your "best friend". Talk to him immediately. That's what friends are for . . .'*

Whatever friendship is, marriage does not guarantee it. Indeed, day-to-day intimacy can make unfriendly demands and stretch beyond limits the tolerance friendships require. It's surprising how many women write to me stunned to discover they have moved in with slobs whom they love, but whose living habits they find self-centred and infuriating. Bathroom etiquette, for example — caps on tubes and tidemarks — can alarm and depress new lovers just as much as it does new flatmates, and prevent them from being friends.

'Do you have a girlfriend?' a busybody asked my son when he was twenty.

'Not at the moment,' he told her, 'but I have lots of friends who are girls.'

It is gratifying to see boys and girls being friends more readily nowadays than was true only a couple of decades ago, or before *that*, when it was practically unknown. Nevertheless, warmth and tolerance are what friends are *for*, and friendship between the sexes continues to be troublesome and elusive in western society, and as good as non-existent elsewhere on the planet.

Someday in a blissful future the sexes, having found a way cheerfully to accommodate lust, will truly be each other's friends, untroubled by jealousy and possessiveness. That will be the day all the agony aunts retire, and the marriage guidance counsellors and family therapists go west; that will be the day everybody is paid according to the job she or he does, housework is equally shared, and abortionists can become paediatricians; that will be the day childhood is always sweet; that will be the day equality is a birth-right. That will be the day. And if you're smart, you won't hold your breath.

The sexes are not very often each other's best friends, and nobody on my side of the postbag could imagine that they want to be, in spite of the peace friendship between them would bring to our troubled communities. Sex requires friction and love between men and women encompasses sex. Sometimes the two sexes make great love, and making great love in the long run has contributed as much to progress, poetry and posterity as being great friends would have done.

A woman writes, *'My best friend and I grew up together. We have always been there for each other. Now she has a new boyfriend and it's getting serious between them. She doesn't call me as much as she used to. He is coming between us and I am broken-hearted . . .'*

I reply, *'Right or wrong, when a young woman meets a man who matters, love comes before everything. It is not the man, it's love that has put a space between you, but only for a while. If you are her good friend, then be happy for her. That's what friends are for. And good friends wait for each other.'*

The friendships of youth are more volatile than they will be later on, precisely because life is volatile, shifting and unsettled. A young girl is bound to have a 'best friend' with whom she shares a bond of sisterhood, almost a blood bond, that is exclusive and intimate. Best friends are allies when girls are disengaging from their families, and they are often shed, understandably though sometimes painfully, as the girls move into new circles of education and work and, of course, new levels of sexual experience.

Girls becoming mature put romance first, as boys do sex, ahead of friendship and practically everything else. That's the way of it. And feelings are hurt among women friends between the ages of about sixteen and twenty as they cannot ever be hurt again. The requirements of same-sex friendship change more radically as we grow older than those of romantic love, which stay more or less the same throughout a lifetime. We have friends for various seasons in our lives. Once in a great golden while, we find a friend for life. But it is in the very nature of some friendships that they have to pass, along with the shared interests or experiences on which they were based.

Sometimes deep friendships pass too, and sometimes — even after years apart — they return to pick up pretty much where they left off. When that happens, when friendship returns to two whom circumstances have parted, it is as magical and full of happiness as any relationship between humans. I believe regaining friendships lost in the hurly-burly is as close as we can come to putting a skip in time's beat.

In theory at least, mature friendships share interests of the mind, the heart, and the neighbourly pursuits of daily life, safe and apart from the burning heat of passion. Women these days who keep smaller households, particularly if we work or are fairly independent, can create whole surrogate families out of friends. On the whole, to see your friends as a family of your own making is an attractive idea, especially in big cities with increasing numbers of divorces and outcasts from broken homes. On the minus side (being an agony aunt compels me to see the bloody minus side of everything), the unresolved patterns of the original families can make a lot of trouble when they are superimposed on a new family made up of friends. In what role, for instance, does the friend-maker cast herself? Dominating mother? Envious sister? Glamorous cousin? Sympathetic and experienced Aunt Agony? According to how they see themselves, and following a bossy script based on unhealed childhood problems, women have been known to attract and cast their friends in roles which sometimes the friends refuse to play, or play badly, or insist on playing their own way.

A woman writes, *'I have known one of my best friends now for fifteen years. We both came from broken homes and had that in common from the start. I used to be overweight and was ridiculed nearly every day at school, and she defended me. After school, I lost weight and got myself together. Now I feel confident in myself. We are still close, but I feel very nervous when I phone her for a chat, afraid she might reject me. Please don't suggest we talk about it. I could never do that.'*

I reply, *'It sounds to me as if you started out playing sisters, the stronger one defending the other from ridicule, as a good sister does. That is a very needy and intense basis for friendship. Now that you have grown up in different ways, the old roles don't fit. Is there a chance for equal give-and-take friendship between you now? If you can't talk about it, I guess not. Talking from the heart is a part of what friends are for. If you can't talk openly, what makes you think you are still friends?'*

When the balance of give-and-take is not in order, or if it shifts, the relationship changes its nature; sometimes it turns envious and nasty. No enemy is ever as keen as a former friend. The ugly duckling, for instance, who emerges as a swan may discover that, along with her dowdy plumage, she has lost some she considered close to her heart. Were they truly friends to begin with? In a way they were, but their loyalty was based on vanity or pity and it could not survive her transformation.

Foul-weather friends are just as unlikely to be loyal when the sun comes out as fair-weather friends are to disappear in the rain. Envy is incompatible with friendship and loyalty. When envy shows, that's when men in particular are heard to say that all women are bitchy and incapable of friendship. The truth is, men are wrong about us (again). In fact women have a special gift for friendship. Heart-to-heart comes easily to us; we are not afraid of intimacy — on the contrary, we stick our necks out for it courageously. Like all special gifts, our friendliness can be a great pain sometimes. The very ease and depth of our intimacies and confidences make a spoiled friendship peculiarly poisonous. There is no enemy as jealous and spiteful as an ex-friend. You can't win them all, but it's worth the risk; when friendships work they are every bit as valuable in a woman's life as love affairs.

One great advantage of a friend over a lover is that grown-ups can have more than one friend, even more than one 'best friend' at a time without being disloyal. While we're on the topic of grown-up friendships, theoretically grown-ups keep their hands off each other's lovers. However, not all adults are grown up, not by a long shot.

A woman writes, *'My best friend's husband has been pursuing me for two years. I find him attractive, but I have no wish to hurt my friend. I value her friendship. I never visit their home without first making sure she is there. He comes to my apartment sometimes, but I refuse to let him in. I don't know whether it's just a game on his part. My resolve is crumbling. I fantasise about him. He says he loves me, but don't they all until they get what they want?'*

I reply, *'There is no way a sane man continues his pursuit unless he senses deep down he's in with a chance. He knows you're interested, otherwise he'd have given up. Take him, lose your friend, and make what you can of your self-respect. Or, on the other hand, retreat from him and, if necessary, from your friend too for a while, until you can look him in the eye, say "get lost", and save your friendship as well as a good opinion of yourself . . .'*

Men disrupt female friendships sometimes, yes. In fact, for a husband or boyfriend to come on strong to his wife's or girlfriend's best friend happens often enough to be practically a cliché in the agony business. I begin to suspect, from the number of letters I receive on the topic, that when a man comes on to his girlfriend's best friend it is not always simply a matter of proximity. Some men flirt mischievously, out of contempt for the feminine values of deep friendships, perhaps. Or maybe they're jealous of the closeness and the confidences between women and feel compelled to spoil it? Or perhaps he is trying to prevent two women from joining forces to 'hex' him? Men are superstitious about female powers. Or maybe the friend is a simulacrum, standing in for the woman he loves but for some reason cannot understand?

Or maybe she isn't a good friend, after all, and has been massaging his knee under the table.

Maybe a guy *shouldn't* make passes at his girlfriend's best friend. If he wrote to me first, I'd tell him he was a disloyal son of a bitch, and a lazy slob into the bargain to look for a little playmate so close to home. And I'd recommend he drop the whole idea before someone who trusts him is doubly hurt: both by him and by one she took for a friend.

Whatever the reason a man comes on strong, and no matter how strong he comes on, any woman who responds to the advances of her friend's lover and lets her 'resolve crumble', is equally disloyal. Even if he has been coming on to her like Ghengis Khan, even 'but I love him', does not change the fact that she is utterly responsible for her own part in whatever happens and will have to suffer her share of the result.

A woman writes, *'My best friend broke up with her boyfriend three months ago. He has started calling me and he's asked me out. I have always liked him, but would I lose my friendship if I accept?'*

I reply, *'In your place, I'd level with her and tell her I was planning to see her "ex". Whether or not you lose your friendship depends upon how their affair ended, and how hurt she was. There is practically bound to be a hiccough between you and her, but it ought to pass in due course. As long as they are well and truly finished with their love affair, he's a free man, and up for grabs. As a point of honour, do your very best never to discuss her with him or him with her.'*

Friendship is a lot more than one-on-one minus sex. We women *will* try to change our lovers and husbands, or wish them closer to a romantic ideal: that is the unfriendliest thing about love affairs. Friends we accept warts and all, and when we can't accept (unless we are spoiled brats or bullies who must have all our own way or nothing) we regulate the extent and depth of the friendship. Unlike lovers, who arrive singly and become obsessions, quite pleasant friends can be taken in small doses.

I have, for example, one friend whom I love dearly and whom I would trust with my life, but to whom I would not dream of entrusting a secret because trying to keep it would half kill her, and she would probably fail. *Should* she keep my secrets for me? Why *should* she? I'm a big girl and I can keep my own.

Approval and disapproval is a traditional familial pastime that has no place between friends. Worry on a friend's behalf, by all means. But we are not each other's keepers. And the moment you start to judge your friend, or she judges you, the friendship is faltering. Make your disapproval public — of her appearance or her personality or the way she raises her children or her taste in men — talk disparagingly about her and without affection to mutual acquaintances, and the friendship, whatever there was of it, is as good as over.

A woman writes, *'After a friend told me my boyfriend was cheating on me, we broke up. We decided to be friends, but it didn't work out as I was upset. A few weeks ago, I went to a party and he was there. He asked for forgiveness. He said he missed me and wanted for us to be friends. I told him I would think about it. My friends tell me I shouldn't get involved with him again, and I feel the same way. Other friends tell me he is miserable without me and still loves me. I am very confused . . .'*

I reply, *'Has it occurred to you that you have too many people you call friends? Try thinking for yourself . . .'*

'Torn', the truth, always assuming it *is* true and what you take it for, counts for no more than what you do with it. You alone know if there are extenuating circumstances that make it imperative to tell your friend what you've seen. But unless your motives are pure, unless you are thinking of nothing at all other than your friend's happiness, unless you feel nothing other than concern on her behalf, in my opinion, keep your own counsel.

If there is the slightest trace of envy, satisfaction, relief or 'I-told-you-so' in your feelings, even just a mere iota, when you see her boyfriend kiss another girl, it doesn't mean you're a bad friend, but it does mean you'd be well advised to mind your own business. Your own business, as far as a good friend is concerned, is keeping lines of communication open between you. If the man she loves is the skunk you take him for (as her friend, you hope he isn't), then before long she is going to need you a lot more than she needs you now to tell her what she does not want to know and, in any case, will not believe.

Spies are a dime a dozen, always ready with bad news, and in the end nobody trusts them; true friends are rare and can be trusted to butt in only when they can do the most good.

• • • • • • • • • •

Dear 'Torn',

Ultimately, whether or not you tell her what you saw is an ethical decision you must make for yourself. All I can tell you is this, chances are she will not believe you or, if she tackles him, he will persuade her that you have an axe to grind and are therefore not a trustworthy informant. You've never liked him, you say, and have made no secret of your feelings. She loves him and makes no secret of her feelings. She's in love, and women in love are predictable only to the degree that they will side with their lover against all odds, all evidence and all criticism.

You say you will not be able to look her in the eyes if you do not tell her what you saw and believe to be his infidelity. In other words, it will make you feel bad if you don't tell her, and it will make her feel bad if you do tell her. In your place I'd choose to feel bad myself rather than hurt my friend. Mind you, if I could, I'd have a word with him — 'Saw you down the club the other night. Do I know the girl you were with . . .?' — and leave it at that. Otherwise, if I were you, I'd hold my tongue for the time being.

As a general rule, bringing a friend bad news about her lover will turn her not against him, but against you. In the midst of her passion she will see your reservations about her lover as jealousy. And later, if he is as bad as you think and shows his true colours to her, chances are she will be too bitter and embarrassed, too afraid to hear 'I told you so', to seek you out when she really needs your concern.

> *Your friend,*
> *Aunt Irma*

• • • • • • • • • •

AGONY AUNT'S WORKSHEET

1. How are 'best friends' different from friends?
2. Name six ways you know you have made a good friend and list them, *least* important first.
3. How many of those six tests of friendship could you apply if the candidate were a gorgeous, heterosexual man?
4. Name three things you would do for a friend and nobody else.
5. Would you do them for a man you fancied?
6. Is there anyone who was a friend but who you no longer speak to, and if so, why do you think she cares?
7. Tell 'Torn' what she should do and why.

PROBLEM NINE

Patterns — you made 'em, who else can break 'em?

• • • • • • • • • •

Dear Irma,

I am twenty-two years old, and after a less than brilliant time at school I found a job working in an animal shelter. My mother says the work is beneath me, but I love it, and I'm thinking about becoming a vet. My dad is always putting me down, too. They don't like my boyfriend because he wears an earring. My sister is the one who can do no wrong. They're throwing a big party for her engagement and I have to go home for it. Whenever I go home it's always the same and I end up feeling miserable for weeks afterwards. It will end up with everybody dumping on me, then I'll get angry as usual, and cry, and feel guilty.

'Stuck'

• • • • • • • • • •

Patterns are what you make of them. Everything is patterns, in fact. We're born into some, some are imposed on us, and some we weave for ourselves as we go, hardly noticing, until one day we look back and see how like we are to spiders, trapped in our own sticky design.

Some patterns are common to particular groups of people. Movie stars choose pretty mates, for example, and divorce practically as often as they marry. Chart one hundred Hollywood marriages and only a few would not follow the identical high-low graph, you can bet on it. Also, people who make a big creative statement in youth rarely top it or equal it later, and so their life's pattern frequently drifts away into a troubled future. As a general rule, men are more prone to criminal patterns of behaviour than women. And in general, women have a greater tendency than men to blame — both others and themselves.

A woman writes, *'He's cold and we hardly ever make love any more. I lie awake all night wondering what I did wrong . . .'*

Another writes, *'We lived together for a year and then he left me for a girl at work. I can't forget him. I go over it and over it in my mind asking myself why I wasn't enough for him . . .'*

And, *'If only I'd taken him back the first time he asked for forgiveness, but I wanted to punish him. I told him to go, and he never came back . . .'*

Blame is a derivative of 'if only', and 'if only' is of course no more than good old feminine wishful thinking, usually in retrospect. Blame joins 'if only' to make an habitual pattern of thought infinitely more dangerous than mere daydreaming, because even though blame often becomes obsessional, it cannot ignite ambition. On the contrary, a woman who is locked into blame mopes around the house, sighing to have things back the way they never were. Blame is the defensive reaction of a weakling who wants things her own way but is afraid to take charge of them. Our tendency to blame ourselves and others, and our stubborn reluctance to move beyond blaming sets us women back into helplessness and dependency.

As for self-blame, if it leads to genuine apology or if it reforms bad behaviour — if it does something constructive, in other words — then long may we continue to feel it, though only when we deserve to. The trouble is, many of the women who write to me blame themselves constantly and persistently for *other* people's bad behaviour, and that is an oddly self-indulgent fallacy which springs from old patterns established back in the days when women felt responsible for everyone, men and children and family: everyone, *except* ourselves.

Blaming herself or others but without energetically correcting anything at all is the way a kid operates. Baby Girl sees herself as the very centre of the universe — how can she know that the space around her is only a nursery? She thinks that what she sees is all there is and it's all hers. Others appear when she cries or calls. A baby cannot imagine that mummy or daddy or anyone makes decisions, or even exists, except in reference to herself. At the same time, she's just a kid, isn't she? Without the force or freedom to do anything very much. Oh, she can *blame*, of course: mummy and daddy when they are not 'there for her', her playmates and sisters for having things she hasn't got, and, in due course, men for treating her in ways she doesn't think they *should*.

Baby Girl blames, and Baby Girl can have a tantrum, too, and she can outgrow the nursery without ever learning to behave any differently. What she does not do, because she thinks she can't, is take charge of her own destiny, and what she doesn't have, because she thinks someone else should be in charge, is a proud sense of responsibility for herself.

When a girl wears a short tight skirt and a skinny lurex top, she isn't asking for trouble, she's asking for admiration. But if she trusts a bunch of strangers in a bar to know the difference simply because they are big strong men and she thinks they *should*, and if she then drinks her inhibitions away, what can I say when she writes to me later asking *me* whether she was raped, because she was too drunk to remember? We cannot have it both ways. If we want practical equality for ourselves and our daughters, then we must break the old pattern of holding big daddy responsible for us no matter how we behave and then blaming him for his failure, when the fact is that men have troubles enough being responsible for themselves and are hardly any better at it than we are.

Are you wondering what I'm rabbiting on about this time? When people complain about a 'pattern' in their letters to me, ten times out of ten they are referring to their own personal lives in the same way that 'Stuck' is, and not to any behaviour pattern of women in general. But an awful lot of the scenarios we set up and repeat to our cost are based on general patterns of behaviour, thought and expectation. Primary among such expectations, even in these more enlightened days, is the belief that men will or *should* take practically total responsibility for our well-being. Then, when the poor guys disappoint us, which they are bound to do, the pattern is to blame men for failing to accomplish what was a half-baked idea in the first place. It is half-baked to give over whole areas of our lives to the care of those who happen to be shaped like daddy.

A woman writes, *'I am an attractive twenty-four-year-old woman who has never had a decent boyfriend. Every guy I go out with uses me, for sex, money or convenience. It has been this way for as long as I can remember. I have a lot of friends who don't understand why I'm still single. I'm starting to be really depressed about my situation. How can I face each day knowing I may never find anyone except the "users" I always fall for?'*
I reply, *'They are not using you. You are using them to help you repeat over and over again a pattern that only you can trace back, understand and stop . . .'*

The patterns of our relationships with men are pretty much based on how we felt about our fathers when we were girls. Believe me, I hate having to say that: it sounds so psuedo-psychotherapeutic. Besides, it irks me to have to believe that one single key can ever open a multitude of secret hearts. But how can I deny what I have observed of my own history and that of practically every woman I have ever known? And I have observed that when a daughter's patterns of love are wonky, daddy has a lot to answer for. Am I blaming him? No. Absent or present, strict or indulgent, faithful or philandering, he has problems of his own, he is not his daughter's problem. He is, however, often part of the explanation.

A woman writes, *'I can't stay away from other women's husbands. I've had an affair with my best friend's husband, a family member's husband, and plenty of other married men. I've never been "in love". I am twenty-five years old, but I cannot stop having relationships with married men. Then it kills me to see them later, out with their wives. How can I break this terrible pattern?'*
I reply, *'Every pattern begins with no more than a dot, the very first point of*

what will become an elaborate repetitious design. First, you have to think back to where the pattern began and recognise why it began. The pattern is your reaction to what started it; you cannot change what started it, but until you know, how can you start to change your reaction? Understanding starts to give you control over what otherwise controls you . . .'

What are patterns for? Everyone develops a set of benign patterns of thought and behaviour that simplify life and make parts of it more predictable, and therefore less threatening. For example, I live in the middle of a big city, I know the patterns of my neighbourhood — Saturday night is noisy and aggressive, lunchtimes are crowded — so I adjust my own patterns of living to accommodate them. In the same way, when you know how various friends are bound to react to a variety of situations, you can adapt your behaviour under certain circumstances to suit theirs, and you can avoid situations which past experience tells you will cause trouble.

Where would we be without a substantial degree of predictable behaviour in ourselves and those around us? Trust is built on predictability as much as on any kind of intuitive understanding. Learning each other's patterns of thought and behaviour allows us to live together with confidence. However, a lot of us find ourselves, like 'Stuck', caught in patterns that hurt us or others or are endlessly destructive as we are compelled to act out the same cursed scenario over and over and over again, hoping to find a happy ending for it at last. Of course, a happy ending eludes us because the problem we keep trying to solve originated in our past, and it was way back then that it failed to find a satisfying conclusion.

A young woman writes, *'My world is confused. I am sixteen and my life has been full of one night stands. I go out with friends and get very drunk. I have found myself in the middle of having sex with a stranger before I realise where I am. Please, please help me.'*
I reply, *'You need a professional guide through this terrible labyrinth so you can emerge from it and put it behind you. Don't be afraid of words like "psychiatrist" or "therapist" or "counsellor". Such people exist precisely to help you. All you need to do is take the first step out towards help . . .'*

Bad patterns can be pathological, and often are. That is not to say, however, that they are incurable. Tracing them back to their source is the beginning of knocking them on the head. There are lots and lots of times when we can do that all by ourselves, but some-times we can use a little help. I do not believe that everyone needs psychotherapy or counselling. However, when a pattern of behaviour proves ungovernable and destructive, and the source of it is hidden or not what it's taken to be, therapy comes into its own.

There are plenty of patterns which are idiosyncratic, odd or uncon-ventional, which in the long run we are better off accommodating, rather than using up precious time in a desperate endeavour to change or break them.

Lil is a great old friend of mine whom I see quite regularly for a meal and a chat. Lil is what's known as a 'soft touch': she gives to charities, to friends when they're broke, and she gives of herself too, always ready to listen, to cherish, and when she must, to forgive. Whenever I invite her for a meal or a drink she arrives laden with gifts for me and my son. Someday, when Lil looks back on the pat-terns of her life, she will see that all her friendships and all her love affairs were shaped like vases from which she poured libations of wine and water.

She and I have analytical, no-holds-barred conversations.

'You know, Lil,' I told her in the course of one of them, 'it could be that you give and give and give because as a child your mother, that cold and critical bitch, deprived you of a sense of self-worth. In other words, my dear, you think nobody will love you if you come to them empty-handed . . .'

'Oh, I've known about all that for ages,' Lil said cheerfully. 'What the hell? Life's short, and nobody's perfect.'

A woman writes, *'I felt left out when all my friends started having boy-friends, so I invented one. That was a year ago, and I have now lied about him so much that they are all keen to meet him, which is, of course, im-possible. I have got away with it by saying he lives in another country. I even write letters to myself, pretending they're from him. I want to stop, but I'm trapped and I hate myself . . .'*

I reply, *'For the first time ever in the history of the Agony column I recom-mend murder. Polish him off. Say he's sent you a breaking-up letter and he's met someone else. To make a pattern, as many do, of lying your way into a desirable position which you have not earned or cannot honestly fill is to pave*

*the road to self-hatred. Put your lie behind you, but remember it, and don't
let it happen again, for it is how patterns begin . . .'*

Of all the words agony aunts use, willpower is at the bottom of the
pit. We live in a time when 'help' is the operative concept, and the
notion that we can hoist *ourselves* out of emotional trouble is greeted
with scorn. And the suggestion that a lot of us would be better off if
we did take responsibility for what ails us can stimulate outrage, as I
have learned more than once when I've thrown a complaining
woman back on her own resources.

Willpower is more soundly out of fashion these days than its close
relative, patience. Yet we want fidelity, don't we? We want success,
we want health, we want love based on more than sex, we want sex
based on more than games of chance; how in blazes do we expect
ever to have any of these good things if we do not exercise willpower
and self-control? If we do not, in other words, take it upon ourselves
to break the patterns that distress us, whether that means fighting together to break disturbing patterns in our society, or fighting all
alone to sweep away patterns in our own lives.

An annual chore which comes the way of agony aunts and our ilk
is what I think of as mopping up after the 'Christmas Crisis', though
to be fair it can happen, as it does to poor 'Stuck', whenever families
get together. All grown up, often with children of their own,
brothers and sisters can slide right back into their old childhood
anxieties, jealousies and pecking order. If the old role-playing were
limited to family gatherings it would be upsetting and demoralising
for a while as it is for 'Stuck', but it would pass quickly. Unfortunately, family patterns have a knock-on effect, particularly in the
lives of women, though men do become trapped in them too.

The role a woman played or plays within her family is very often
the one she casts herself in at work, or so it seems to me from the
letters I receive where childhood difficulties are superimposed on the
office or shop floor situation. Mummy's pet, daddy's pet, resentful
scapegoat sister, black sheep: it is surprising how often letters con-
cerning problems in the workplace translate into family patterns.

A woman writes, *'Nobody in my office likes me. I think it's because I can
often see what needs to be done before the rest do . . .'*

Another says, *'I can't seem to hold a job for more than a little while before'*

*everyone starts taking advantage of my good nature and expecting me to do
more than my share of work . . .'*

Or, *'I have to keep changing jobs because the bosses make passes at me . . .'*

And, *'They all criticise me and talk about me behind my back . . .'*

Once any pattern has started operating in the office, the way to
change it, or end it, is to stop playing your role there, often the very
one you played at home, and find one more appropriate to work.
Don't be stuck-up sis who competes for parental praise, don't even
want to be; don't be good old sis who does the dishes every night,
don't allow yourself to be; don't flirt with daddy — don't let the boss
make a pass, and if he's fool enough to try, handle it without needing
to leave your job — if you're the outsider, treat the insiders with
courtesy, but why worry about their opinion of you? You are in control of it; *their* preconceptions will change according to *your*
behaviour.

Habits are small patterns within bigger ones. The habitual alcoholic, for example, can plot out his day according to drinks, and all
those sodden days make up the bigger pattern of an alcoholic life.
When a habit rules it becomes addiction. The pattern of addiction is a
spiral, dizzying and downward. Drink, drug, or consoling chocolate,
only for the time when she is actually using it does the addict stop
wanting it. Immediately afterwards, she wants her drink, drug or
calories again, worse than ever. The original need, whatever it was,
which drove her to the drink, the drug, the food, the habit, the pattern, in the first place is replaced by a need for the drink, the drug,
the food, the habit, the pattern itself. Drugs, in other words, become
what you take them for. And the bad pattern becomes, again and
again, whatever started it in the first place.

Addictions can be treated. Patterns can be broken. But no matter
how strong is the treatment, how tender the care, how understanding the counsellors, the power of your own will must pertain.
Two-thirds of willpower is desire. Know your pattern, know its
source, stop blaming anyone else for it, stop blaming yourself, only
want to end it, want with all your might to stop it. Then dig your
heels in, summon wanting and will, and fight for your life.

• • • • • • • • • •

Dear 'Stuck',

The moment you go home they cast you as the child you were and you, obligingly, behave the way you used to do: you fight, you resent, you get angry, you sulk and feel guilty. Well, this time, don't play. You know you love your job, you know you can make a career out of it if you work hard. You know your boyfriend counts for more than his earring. Your family does not know these things and why should they? You're leading your life, not theirs. And for what it's worth, it sounds to me as though you are doing a very good job of it, too.

Surprise them. Go in smiling. Hear their judgements with a shrug. Take the old pattern into your own two hands and break it. Do you know how we break the patterns of childhood? We grow up.

Yours truly,
Aunt Irma

• • • • • • • • • •

AGONY AUNT'S WORKSHEET

1. What would you say is the difference between something that is your fault and something that is your responsibility?

2. Name three responsibilities, *least* important first, that all of us have in common.

3. Choose three patterns of your own behaviour, no matter how benign or insignificant — eating habits, say, or the way you act in a crowd — and trace them back to their source or as close as you can come to it.

4. Choose a habit or characteristic you would like to change and then give not one, not two, but three good reasons why you do not do so.

5. Think of three people you know well and draw the pattern of their love-lives: peaks, valleys, circles, break ups, and so on.

6. When your family gathers, describe the role each member plays.

7. Frame a reply to 'Stuck'.

PROBLEM TEN

Life stinks — why?

•••••••••

Dear Irma,

  I'm just a big nothing. When I was younger my little sister was better at everything. My parents have always told me I should be more like my sister. They find fault with everything I do. I'm twenty-one. I live at home, and my father still calls me 'the fat slob'. I need to lose around twenty pounds, but I can't. I have a job I hate, I'm not qualified for anything else. My boyfriend treats me bad. My last boyfriend of two years went off with my best friend. All I want is to feel good about myself like other girls. I can see my whole life going on this way. I get so unhappy I consider suicide to end it all. Please help.

'A Nobody'

•••••••••

I long to take that fashionable phrase 'feeling good about myself' and erase it from language and memory. I'd be a very happy agony aunt if I never had to read it ever again.

'Feeling good about myself' is another new cliché, and a cliché, new or old, is a dopey way to say something that feels sort of, vaguely, like, almost right, at the end of the day, when all is said and done: know what I mean? Use a cliché and it means you can stop thinking, thinking about what's at stake, thinking about what you, and only you, want to say for yourself.

I've taken against the very sound of 'feeling good about myself': you come over as self-centred and smug if you do 'feel good about yourself', and if you don't, if you 'feel bad about yourself', you sound weepy and self-pitying. What I like least of all is its ring of unmitigated selfishness: 'I feel really good about myself' manages to suggest that someone else probably feels lousy, and who cares? If ever I've heard a phrase that muddles self-importance with self-respect, it has to be 'feeling good about myself'. Maybe for the few moments while a spoiled-brat movie star trashes a hotel room he 'feels good about himself'. Maybe a beauty queen feels good about herself as she is being raised over her competitors, but not for long. No doubt Hitler felt good about himself. 'Feeling good about myself' gives the idea of a finished job, thank you very much. But, in truth, acquiring self-esteem — which is as close as anyone needs to come to 'feeling good about herself' — and hanging on to it, is a full-time pursuit.

Self-esteem does *not* come from 'feeling good about yourself', damn it. Self-esteem comes when you forget all about yourself and feel good about other people, feel good about tomorrow morning, feel good *in* yourself: feel good.

'Respect' has recently become a dangerous concept in the United States, where it is persistently confused with 'obedience'. The street slang 'disrespect' or 'dis', as in 'he dissed me, so I shot him', is slipping into everyday language. And 'respect your mother' these days no longer means to treat her with special regard and courtesy; it is instead taken to be practically the same as saying 'obey her'. Does that mean a child must sacrifice self-respect in respect of (obedience to) a tyrannical or irrational mother? I certainly would hate to give anyone that idea. Nothing is as destructive to a sense of self as blind or mindless obedience to what is abhorrent.

'Self-respect' is becoming practically meaningless except in a severely critical sense: 'If you had any self-respect, you'd never sleep with a stranger . . .', or 'If he had any self-respect, he'd cut his hair . . .' Every time 'A Nothing's' father, the wretch, calls her 'You fat slob . . .', he implies harshly, 'Have you no self-respect?' And the poor girl can only hang her head and reply, 'None. Where was I supposed to get it from, daddy?'

All in all, when I address myself to 'A Nobody', I'll stick with 'self-esteem', a more gentle concept these days, meaning simply a fair and good opinion of oneself, less vexed and loaded than 'self-respect'. Self-esteem can never derive from comparisons with others, least of all physical comparisons. If it could, how would any woman ever achieve self-esteem as long as the world has Cindy Crawford in it? For that matter, how would Cindy Crawford hang on to her self-esteem in a world where her own image is enhanced way, way beyond the reflection she wakes up to in her mirror? Cindy Crawford, in other words, is not *quite* Cindy Crawford, as who knows better than she? She cannot escape her image, she has to see it every day of her life, glorified and never growing older, looking down from every second billboard to remind her of what she is not *quite*.

Not many years ago we women squawked to high heaven about how dehumanising it was that men saw us merely as sex objects. Well, after all this time on my side of the agony postbag, I begin to suspect we are equally guilty of seeing ourselves as objects: objects of fashion, objects of envy, objects of sex, too — or, more specifically, gleaming and impenetrable objects of desire. When so very many women who write to the Agony column are willing to lodge their confidence and good opinion of themselves mainly in how they look — and I know from letters just how many thousands of young women are increasingly doing precisely that — then it requires no more than a little common sense to figure out that the men who come on to them will also be interested mainly in their looks.

A woman writes, *'I am thinking about having cosmetic surgery to enlarge my bust, but I'm rather worried about it . . .'*
I reply, *'All I can say is that there are as many fulfilled and happy flat-chested women in this world as there are miserable C-cups . . .'*

Of course I realise that looks have always accounted for the big 'Wow!' and turn of a man's head, and I'd be an idiot to pretend life is a bowl of cherries for girls with no confidence whatsoever in their allure. However, it is we women who set most of the standards for what is fashionable and attractive; men in general go for what's on offer. Very few men care what a woman wears unless it's too tight, or not tight enough. It is not what you wear but the way you wear it that turns heads.

Free to find ourselves, boldly to create our own self-confidence, lovingly to nurture our own self-esteem, and at last to do all any of us *can* to uncover our own idiosyncratic charms and deepest virtues, instead our feminine notions of what's beautiful have become more exclusive than ever, more strict, unimaginative, authoritarian and plastic.

Young women are racing to lace themselves into constricting, narrow-minded, glossy, corny definitions of how they should look, and they are refusing to acknowledge how many divinely different shapes beauty can take in human form — some of them plump, some with downy upper lips, some with flat chests, and a whole lot of them with cellulite. Here's a funny thing. Seven-eighths of the multitude of complaints about their appearance which my correspondents allow to become an agony, are tiny flaws that your average sexy guy would barely notice, by which he would certainly not be put off his stroke once he was close enough to see, and might even find kind of cute. I have before me, for example, a photograph of a girl that came enclosed in her letter complaining that facial hair is 'ruining my sex life'. I have studied this glossy snapshot, I've squinted and peered at it, and I can see nothing except a fresh, young, pretty face. There is perhaps just a trace of a downy upper lip, but I needed a magnifying glass to see it, and in some societies it would be considered a madly sexy attribute.

Another woman writes, *'When I was young, I had emergency surgery on my stomach. I have a seven-inch scar that will stay for the rest of my life. I can never wear a bikini. I feel so sad and bad about myself.'*

Scars that are not to any noticeable degree disfiguring, facial hair, dimples, veins, an inch of flesh here or there, concave nipples, convex navels, freckles, thick ankles, thin arms, even once a woman with unequal earlobes — you name it and someone somewhere has written in to an agony aunt to say it is ruining her sex life and preventing her from 'feeling good about herself'.

Of course, there's always plastic surgery and I guess I could have recommended it to the girl with the scar on her stomach, and to a lot of others. But surely she and the thousands of others who write to complain of minor imperfections cannot all be so shallow, so image-obsessed, so timid, as to allow their confidence and self-esteem and joy in life to be ruined by a physical characteristic, barely visible to others, and nothing more than one of the countless ways that nature shapes a healthy human body?

Like the anorexic literally dying of starvation and weeping in agony because she ate a banana and gained an ounce, so the girl in deep despair over a scar on her belly and blaming it for all that is wrong in her life *must* be merging superficial, half-imagined blemishes with darker and more profound insecurities. I will not believe otherwise of a generation of women I have come to understand and cherish.

We women have not been designed by nature primarily to appear on the cover of *Cosmopolitan* magazine. And those few who are the fashion flavour of the month or the year are not automatically happy as a result. True enough, Cindy Crawford has never written to me in agony (at least I don't think she has) and I hope she never feels the need to do so. But it is surprising how many stunning beauties do write to agony aunts or cry on friends' shoulders because they lack confidence in themselves, and are snake-belly low in self-esteem. Believe me, I have read the heartaches of pretty women so often, I am convinced that wherever a girl looks for her self-esteem, a mirror is one of the last places she'll find it. And if she allows herself to be so vain that she does find it there, she won't have it for long. The great late stretch of her life will be bitter with loss.

'Dear Irma, friends tell me I am beautiful, so why . . .?'

'I am a model and guys are always hitting on me, so why . . .?'

'I'm not being vain when I say I'm pretty, so why, why, why don't I feel good about myself?'

Fair enough, a beauty turns heads when she walks into a room. But they are not seeing *her*: they are seeing how she looks. It is practically impossible for a beauty to be seen as anything *else*, only beautiful. And any girl who thinks it must be fun to be seen only for her beauty, needs her wee little head examined. When it comes to the long, stable love-life and family-life most women want in the end, beautiful women have such a bad track record it has to be said that extreme good looks can actually blight a poor girl's chances of long-term contentment.

Not only must high-gloss beauty pass awfully fast, but the eyes of a lover soon become accustomed to it, and if that is what drew him in the first place, he will immediately start trying to find it again, somewhere else.

The high-profile lovers who attach themselves to famous beauties are the stuff of every girl's daydreams, I guess. But I can't be alone in noticing that, by and large, a man who goes for a gorgeous girl is either one of those rich collectors of pretty women, along with other pretty things, or is himself a professional glamourpuss, and therefore just as dependent on public admiration for self-esteem, as vulnerable to changes in fashion, and equally shaky inside. The majority of perfectly able-bodied, sexy, humorous, adorable men, though they may do a double-take for a beauty, will turn away from her to have and hold someone more approachable and *human*, someone who is less of a trophy, someone possessed of intimate allure: a girl who is not so all-fire dazzling to every man who passes.

I have nothing against models, by the by. One of my dearest friends used to be a famous model, and she is still one of my dearest friends. But models are there to be looked at, quite simply, and they are essentially expected to be no more than gorgeous clothes-hangers. Granted, top-flight girls are paid a fortune — overpaid, in fact — but they know nothing of personal achievement or self-esteem acquired the only way it can be, I'm afraid, steadily and slowly; they know nothing much at all of life or work compared to a waitress, say, or a mother of toddlers, a teacher, a brain surgeon, a student or a taxi driver. Besides, for the majority of models by far, their fabulous career amounts to a series of boring, badly paid jobs and a stream of disappointments. Show me a model at thirty-plus, and with very few exceptions (two? three?) I'll show you a has-been. Models are not in any sense great role models.

The whole concept of 'role models' is in any case very questionable. It is herself a young woman needs to find, not some imitation Barbie who is already an imitation of an imitation of an imitation of beauty. In fact, it is herself and nobody else that a woman who wants fulfilment has to free from *every* stereotype, and in the end, even the most worthy 'role models' are merely new stereotypes.

Is it any wonder I am alarmed by the recent increase in letters from girls who dream only of being butterflies?

A woman writes, *'Dear Irma, all my friends agree I ought to be a model. How do I start . . .?'*

Do you know how often I am asked? On average, twenty times a month. They're asking *me*? How in hell would I know? Many of them enclose photographs, and they are all pretty. Perhaps one or two that I've seen over the years, given the breaks, could become a professional clothes-horse. I don't know. But I know enough to recognise that eight or nine out of ten are fooling themselves. Self-delusion, that mischievous enemy of promise, smiles out of their hopeful faces: they are not tall enough, or conventionally cute enough, or young enough, or fashionably gaunt enough to make it in the cold crass terms of modelling. If it is confidence in themselves they want to find (and to a girl, that is precisely what they hope to find) they will have to look for it somewhere else, not in the fickle eye of an admiring public.

'If you must have your inexperienced hearts broken,' I want to tell them, 'then let love do it for you, not vanity.'

A woman writes, *'My current boyfriend cheats on me, I know. But as long as I have this scar on my stomach, what other guy will ever go for me . . .?'* **I reply,** *'Call it your "glad to be alive" scar, and any guy who doesn't want to kiss it for your own sweet sake is closer than he deserves to be. It's not the scar, it is your whole self you need to start working on right away, so that you wake up one day to see straight past the weightless reflection in your mirror to the real, solid, loving, good woman within.*

As for the man you love, or the one who will love you in the future, do you expect him always and only to watch you in a mirror as well? Lovers look into each other's eyes, they always will, and that will always be where they see who is at home.'

Don't get me wrong. I like clothes, and I wear makeup. I am not a crotchety spoilsport railing against self-beautification. Never before have so many cosmetics and beauty aids been available over the counter: that's a good thing, that's great, that's terrific, that makes the world a prettier and more amusing place. If any brunette wants to know life as a blonde or a redhead, why not? When a blemish is worrying and it can be healed or removed, then by all means get rid of it. If someone has had reason for as long as she can remember to suffer over her nose, or earlobes, or whatever, and she can afford to do something about it, then let her get on with it and good luck to her. When there is a genuine disfigurement or deformity that modern techniques can correct and the sufferer is in a position to have it done, for heaven's sake, what's stopping her?

Only it is folly for a girl with, say, a scar on her belly to imagine that commitments, responsibilities, the quality of love, or anything else of more importance than a bikini line will change just because she has a few inches of puckered skin repaired. Until she is sure of that within herself, plastic surgery is bound to end in disappointment.

Experts abound to give women advice about their looks, and help us make the best of them. Thanks be to God, that is not my job. An agony aunt doesn't need to come up with anything stylish. On the contrary, my job is distinctly unfashionable: helpful busybodies like me are required only to remind others of what they already know for themselves — what we all know, have known, and will know deep down long after today's way of thinking is lining the cat's litter tray.

My job, such as it is (you can do it for yourselves), is to keep telling you that miracles are more than skin-deep. There is always a deeper, less seasonal, more logically sane reason for any girl's gut-wrenching lack of joy in life than, for example, her reluctance to be seen in a bikini. An agony aunt, or any helpful friends, can only amplify the whisper of her inner voice, so that the troubled person says, 'Of course! I guess I knew that all the time!'

I suppose some would say I am a professional spoilsport (you can do *that* for yourselves, too, and how!). Naturally, I prefer to think that seeing past the mirror image actually removes the shadow of passing fancies and reveals joy, pure, infinitely bright and accessible.

A woman writes, *'Irma, my boyfriend is always putting me down in public, which is ruining my confidence in myself. Also he is very jealous and whenever I try to look nice for a special party, he says I'm dressed like a tramp.'*

The people we love buck us up and remind us when we're low of how perfectly wonderful we are. We do the same for them, don't we? But I'm afraid it is worse than nothing to hand responsibility for your self-esteem to another and expect him (it's usually a him) to take it on cheerfully. The burden is unfair and more than love can be required to bear. As a rule, any woman who is so deficient in self-esteem that she has to expect it to be provided by her boyfriend will in the end receive only a reinforcement of her own low opinion of herself.

Men have troubles of their own in the self-esteem department (perhaps you've noticed?), and when a woman doesn't think much of herself, then the odds must increase that she will attract a man whose confidence is also pretty low, though he may try to hide it behind bluster and boasting.

'What a lowlife jerk I must be,' says his inner voice, *'to stay with a woman whose opinion of herself is so low, she thinks she can't do better than a lowlife jerk like me . . .'*

Or, *'She must be flirting with all those other guys; every one of them is a better provider with a bigger cock than mine . . .'*

Or, *'She's the most wonderful woman I've ever met. But if I don't keep putting her down in public, she might start to realise how great she is, and then she will want to leave a miserable worm like me and find someone better . . .'*

The feast one low self-esteem can make of another low self-esteem is nowhere more evident than when men beat the women they live with. How can any man who holds a good opinion of himself live with a woman who thinks so little of herself that she'll stay put and let a ham-fisted jerk knock her around? It's not possible. Whether he's a university professor or an unemployed trucker, any big person who beats a smaller person holds a very low opinion of himself, and for good reason: he really is a ham-fisted jerk. That's *his* problem. But the woman who stays with a ham-fisted jerk holds an equally low, or lower, opinion of what she is worth, or why would she stay with him? And that is *her* problem.

A woman writes, *'Irma, I've tried and tried to leave him. But he always comes after me, crying and promising he'll never hit me again. Sometimes he is very good to me. And I love him. We've been together for three years. We have a two-year-old daughter . . .'*

Why does any woman stay with a violent man, or return to him? Partly, because it seems easier to cringe together than to be scared alone. And also because the rages or humiliations or beatings reinforce and express what the couple feel about each other and themselves: 'love', they call it — I'd call it a sort of passionate mutual contempt. One way or another, beater and beaten have an investment in the violence continuing: if they regained control of themselves suddenly, even if just one of them did, and the beatings stopped, there is every chance they'd find they had no further need or desire to stay together.

And if there turns out to be abiding affection and sheltering love under the ugly beatings, a couple will not see it or be able to use it until they have cured the violence. It's possible to do this intelligently, through forthright discussion and analysis — perhaps with professional help, and only out of striking reach. Violence *can* be treated, but only from a safe distance.

Men and women, and especially their children, are better off out of a home as long as it contains physical violence. And those who stay in violent relationships, whatever their excuses, whatever their rationale, are afraid: afraid of loneliness, afraid of tenderness, afraid to lose themselves in love, afraid to speak, afraid to ask for help, afraid to know their own worth. They will never learn self-confidence or acquire maturity and dignity until the hitting stops.

Worst of all, those who beat and allow themselves to be beaten will pass an inextricable tangle of weakness, brutality and love right on down the line, a sad and dangerous inheritance for their children. Before 'A Nobody' expects to find her self-esteem by way of a man, she had better stoke her opinion of herself up high enough to attract and be attracted to confident men, who feel secure in the company of confident women. When she has at last stepped out, tall and proud of herself, she will be able to put an end to unwholesome affairs with guys who cheat or treat her badly. As long as 'A Nobody' continues in her low opinion of herself, however, she will go on choosing men who are driven to keep her craven and servile and low in order to reinforce the low opinion they have of themselves. Involuted? You bet. Basically, it's simply this: like attracts like, only they don't necessarily *look* alike.

While 'A Nobody' has me thinking on this squiggly line, I'll add that it is quickly evident even to a not very bright or sensitive man when a woman has low confidence in herself. In spite of all she does to hide low self-esteem, it will out. Even if she tries to cover it up, as women often do, with loads of makeup and flamboyant clothes, he'll soon sense it; after all, it's what he's been on the lookout for, and what he needs. The neediness of her poor self-confidence will show itself in an insatiable hunger for crumbs of praise, say; in her despairing jealousy if he so much as glances at another girl; in the plans she makes but never carries through; in her empty threats and futile attempts to leave him; and mostly in the way she allows herself to be treated by a creep such as he knows himself to be, and still she stays around for more.

I have always detested the phrase 'loving too much'. The concept is cold, selfish and essentially mean-spirited. There is no limit to love and no measure. Women who stay when a situation is actually intolerable do not love too much: they do not love themselves enough to believe their love is worth much at all, so how can they love him, or anyone, 'too much'?

'My parents still tell me I should be more like [my sister],' says 'A Nobody'. Countless others write, too, who say as she does that their mothers have always underrated them, their fathers jeered, their siblings surpassed them, their parents neglected them. And it is true, all of it is probably true. As long as we're children where else can we look if not to our parents for confidence and self-esteem? The trouble is, our mums and dads often are looking to *us*, their children, for exactly the same things. An awful lot of parents see their offspring as continuations of themselves, to carry on and extend their own ambitions or, just as likely, to make good their own disappointments. Growing up involves rejecting roles we genuinely do not want to play: this is the first hard job anybody's kids have to do, or they go under, and unless parents are perfect, it can be a very noisy, painful business.

Perfect parents in a perfect world would guide, instruct, explain, encourage, and never, never criticise. They would acknowledge each child's virtues instead of her flaws; they would see her as lovable, and tell her so; they would treat her as an individual and not a carbon copy of their unrealistic ideal; they would help her reveal her own true gifts bit by bit and admire her as a great discovery, not merely show her off as their own invention.

Perfect parents would cultivate, not suppress; they would be ever on the alert for happy surprises and never know disappointment. Perfect parents would never choose to abandon a child, under any circumstances — in a perfect world they would never need to. And for no reason whatsoever — *no reason whatsoever* — none — at *any* point along the way, would perfect parents break off communication with their children.

In a perfect world, respect would be mutual and disobedience would not signify: what rules existed would all be reasonable. Perfect parents would accept, though with concern, all choices made by their adult children. (Having raised them perfectly, of course, in a perfect world, and filled them with self-esteem, they would have less reason for anxiety than less perfect parents.)

In a perfect world, love would be having to say 'I'm sorry' whenever it needed to be said: perfect parents would apologise when they made a mistake, but never, never say 'I told you so!'

There are no perfect parents, of course. Never were. This is not a perfect world. Not yet. And maturity always begins with an act of forgiveness.

Way back in the fifties, when psychoanalysis was coming into fashion, and for a long time afterwards, our old folks took the blame for absolutely everything from an overbite, to PMT, to adult sexual malfunction. In spite of recent public revelations of child abuse in general and a few specific celebrity revelations (rather self-gratifying in the main), it seems from what I read in my postbag that young people are now easing up on mum and dad a little. Could that be in part because marriages so often break down in modern life that parents and step-parents are all a-muddle in lots of cases? Also, society itself is more and more resembling an old-fashioned parental force, so pervasive are its values and fashions, so insistent and persuasive. Opinions and warnings and points of view every bit as authoritarian and bossy as mum's and dad's ever were are coming at us constantly across the airwaves and via print and film.

'He still calls me "the fat slob",' says 'A Nobody'. I want to wash the old boor's mouth out with carbolic soap. How dare he insult his own flesh and blood as he would not risk a bloody nose to insult a stranger? He must have a very bad opinion of his own flesh and blood: himself, in other words. Take it as read, bullies are always cowards without any real sense of self-worth. 'A Nobody' cannot go back into the past and change her parents, or *their* parents, or indeed anything, but somebody must right away make a tremendous effort and break the leaden chain of low self-esteem that weighs down the generations.

Come on, 'A Nobody', let that somebody be you!

On the whole, readers are easier on each other than I am. There was the time, for example, when a woman wrote to me whose husband had expressed interest in sleeping with her and her sister, whereupon she invited her sister home for a boozy evening and then shared the marital bed with her, leaving her husband on the sofa. She was subsequently 'horrified and distressed' when she woke up and found her husband next to her, having the time of his life.

I still ask myself why she did not put her sister on the sofa instead of into her husband's half of the bed? To set up the ideal scenario for a fantasy he'd already expressed several times, and then be furious when he took advantage of what he may easily have mistaken for an invitation was pretty feeble in my book, and so I told her. Immediately, there fell upon my head a deluge of letters from furious women: did I mean to say that the wronged wife, or any woman, had the slightest responsibility for his beastly behaviour, or any man's?

Yes, as a matter of fact, that was precisely what I meant to say: to the degree that we are responsible for our own behaviour in matters sexual and what the outcome of it is likely to be. There are no reasons except childish ones for any woman to expect any man to be more controlled or strong-willed than she. She was drunk? So was he. She lost control? So did he. He behaved like a selfish ninny? She was one, too.

If we rely on the other guy to be in control of sexual situations, and to control himself because we think he *should*; if we surrender control of ourselves and what's going on, then we're right back in the bad old days of danger and dependence, with nobody to blame for losing ground but you-know-who.

Of course, I always assume that the women who write to me *want* to be adult and responsible for themselves; perhaps that is a failure of imagination on my part? For I cannot conceive of anyone choosing a dependency or actually preferring to ride pillion, and if there are young women out there so wasteful of their lives and so eager to hand them over to someone else, I hope they know better than to write to me. It has also happened that when I feel a troubled person like 'A Nobody' deserves a lot of sympathy, there are those out there who will write in to disagree.

A woman writes, *'Dear Irma, I think you were wrong to encourage the girl* *who wrote about her lack of self-worth. Why doesn't she just look around at others who are worse off than she is and stop being so selfish?'*

I would not dream of telling 'A Nobody' to look at those worse off than herself. For one thing, it wouldn't work — it never does. And besides, if comparing herself to others in trouble did make her 'feel good about herself', then she would be in danger of an even deeper trouble. There is *never* any reason for self-satisfaction, *everything* anyone does could have been done differently, or as well, or is not yet finished. To be self-satisfied is to be self-deluded, and it is not a secure foundation for one's own self-confidence and self-esteem.

Self-satisfaction, by the by, also happens to be an occupational hazard for agony aunts. To make a point of looking at those worse off than yourself with anything in mind except their trouble — be it gold stars in your celestial chart, or 'feeling good about yourself', or 'feeling better about yourself' — is very, very dangerous. Anyone who thinks she wants to help others (or herself) must beware of self-satisfaction, for it can seduce her even as she is in the midst of doing a service, *especially* then, and coat her good intentions with the greasiest kind of pity. Yeuch!

As problem-solving goes (including your own), it is in general more helpful to cultivate anger than pity.

A woman writes, *'At the age of twenty, my life is a mess. I am plagued with feelings of envy over a college friend who is popular and attractive. Her latest man is my ex-fiancé. I don't want to lose her friendship, but I feel more and more insignificant whenever I am with her. How will I come to terms with it?'*

I reply, *'Is she a good friend, this woman who is dating your former fiancé? See a lot of her, do you? She confides her problems in you, does she? And asks your advice about makeup? Frankly, she doesn't sound like much of a friend to me. Don't worry about coming to terms with your envy of her. Why should you? The attempt just provides you with a great excuse for feeling inferior. Get away from her and other gloomy reminders. Put yourself in new places where life comes to terms with you . . .'*

The other side of self-satisfaction is envy: eye-smarting, frown-inducing, bile-churning, bad-tempered, mean-spirited envy, the most spiteful, tricky and incapacitating of all our non-essential emotions, and the great destroyer of friendships and families. Envy sucks. And there is a hell of a lot of it around, too. 'A Nobody' says her parents keep telling her to be more like her sister. Parents frequently say this kind of thing to their children; it beats me why. Obviously, it's bound to do more harm than good, engendering self-hatred and envy.

On top of all the rest, envy is not related to generous admiration or energetic ambition; it's a narrow, lazy-making feeling, which accomplishes nothing worthwhile, and is bound to do the very opposite of what 'A Nobody's' parents, for instance, would say they want for their daughter when they compare her to her more successful sister. Why bother looking for Mr Wonderful, whines envy. The best guys go for *her*, not me. Why try to do anything worthwhile? My parents will always prefer my sister anyhow. Why diet? She has the bones. Why try? *She* wins the prizes.

Envy can be outspoken, or tricky, phoney and smarmy, but whenever it names another, 'the bitch' is understood. Because sooner or later, it never fails to happen that envious people begin to imagine that the ones they envy have stolen something that would otherwise rightfully be their own, and then they sink back into malevolence and a sulky lethargy: 'Why bother getting off my ass?' asks envy. 'She's grabbed everything I ever wanted, the bitch!'

A woman writes, *'Dear Irma, there is this girl who comes into a bar where I go. She's blonde, and she always wears tight, bright clothes. This man friend of mine told me the other day that the guys all talk about her. It makes me so mad they're talking about my acquaintance like that. Should I tell her what they say about her behind her back . . .?'*
I reply, *'As a general rule in this life, whenever the phrase "for her/his/your/ their own good" attaches itself easily in your mind to any action on behalf of another, you're about to do something despicable.'*

When envy is based on no more than another woman's bigger boobs or longer lashes, when it is based on nothing more than someone else's dumb good luck, when it is based on what could more constructively be admired than envied, or when it is based on nothing very much, then the envious person can bring willpower, control and judgement to bear on envy, just as she would on any other destructive habit. As soon as she finds the confidence to see the one she envies clearly, not darkly, not greenly, not merely as a yardstick for herself, but as a sister or fellow in this life, then she may well discover she actually quite likes the person she's been envying. 'A Nobody', for example, could discover that her sister is her ally in the family, and waiting to be friends. Best friends have been known to grow out of envy. How can anyone continue bitterly to envy another she likes and admires? She can't. It's not logical. And I don't give two figs what anyone says, logic changes our minds and touches our hearts, too.

On the other hand, if after honest and unprejudiced consideration you (let's say it's you) find you genuinely do not like her whom you envy, then go ahead and dislike her; that's allowed. But if you genuinely dislike her for good reasons, that means you must be envying her for *bad* reasons. So cut it out.

Easier said than done? Yes. What isn't? But don't let that stop you.

The straightforward path is where the solution lies, as often as not. It is also, however, a very dull and unenlightening way to arrive at an answer. Wandering down byways keeps an agony aunt on her toes and increases her weaponry for future use. Anyhow, there has to be an exchange of insights beyond the frame of the problem in hand and some fun too in agony auntying, you know, or where would job satisfaction come from? Except *in extremis* or in church, solemnity is quite often a pompous fraud. Sometimes the best thing you can do for a troubled friend is to take her out of herself for a little while, to a movie perhaps, or a concert, make her smile, pour her a stiff drink. Maybe if 'A Nobody' were here with me right now, I'd invite her out to try on hats. A couple of women trying on hats together is always good for a laugh; laughter cleans the palate for hope and is one of the best temporary cures for misery I know. The best of all is home-made chicken soup.

'But, Auntie Irma, enough already of where my self-esteem is NOT,' I can hear 'A Nobody' (and you) cry. 'Where IS it?'

'In you', is the only answer. 'Rummage around, and you will find it.'

'If we could but see ourselves as others see us . . .' has always struck me as a witless thing to say. In fact, others see us pretty much as we see ourselves, and thus a lot of self-confidence springs from a confidence trick. Think yourself sexy, others see you as sexy; think yourself on top of it, they see a woman on top of it; think shy and shy is what they'll take you for.

How the girls who write to me in crises of confidence want to be seen is up to them. But the most persuasive conmen have to persuade themselves first of all. Who can sell the Brooklyn Bridge as convincingly as the man who's dead sure he owns it and it's really his to sell? By that token, the most attractive and appealing image any woman can project is the one she knows to be the true one, the one she holds comfortably, the one she has worked patiently to find, the one that was revealed to her as her real self, after doubts and resentments and fears had been acknowledged and discarded.

'A Nobody' cannot look outside herself to others and expect them to deliver her sense of self and self-worth. Pride is stored within. The keys to unlock it, however, are to be found in the big world. What she chooses to *do* with herself and *make* of her life is how she will discover (and invent) her pride. Once 'A Nobody' summons up the energy to begin her exploration of the possibilities, there will be no magic, not right away: for a long time, there will only be hard work and it requires patience. You remember patience, don't you, 'A Nobody', that dreary old virtue that we hoped to put away with thrift and chastity?

A young woman writes, *'Dear Irma, I am in love with a forty-year-old man who works with my father. He is married but he says he will leave his wife as soon as their kids have grown up. Do you think there's hope for us? I know I'm only sixteen but everyone says I am really mature for my age . . .'*
I reply, *'He's a cradle-snatcher, a cad and a villain. If you were the least bit grown-up you would see that for yourself. Do you know what it means to be mature for your age at sixteen? It means to be seventeen . . .'*

A woman writes, *'Dear Irma, I never want to have children. I'm twenty, old enough to know I'm going to devote myself to my career. I've been trying to find a doctor to sterilise me, but so far I've had no luck. Do you know where I can find one?'*
I reply, *'If I did, I wouldn't tell you . . .'*

Another young woman writes, *'I am sixteen and want to have a baby. My boyfriend is seventeen and does not really want a child, but we have been trying for one as he loves me and wants me to be happy. I have never had such* *strong feelings about anything except having a baby. Please tell me I'm doing the right thing . . .'*

I reply, *'How can I? The reasons for wanting a baby are part of your in-heritance and will be with you for many years to come. The reasons for having a baby, however, are to give it security, a stable home, a promising future and eventually to give it freedom. You are not able to do any of those things . . .'*

Another says, *'I am eighteen and have a daughter of eight months. I live at the top of my grandparents' house. My fiancé works some distance away so I only see him once or twice a month. My problem is I get so bored. I miss the life of a teenager. Is there a way I can live my life as an eighteen-year-old, having fun, learning, even with a baby . . .?'*

I reply, *'You are no longer an eighteen-year-old girl, you are an eighteen-year-old mother. You can no longer be the centre of your own life because your baby has taken that place: it is hers by rights . . .'*

If there is a single dangerous weakness evident in most of the young women who write to me, it is their tearing hurry to lock doors — their fearful lack of patience, their wonky sense of how time works. In due course, time has us all. Why hurry to rush the process?

Young people who write to me have very odd ideas about time. Sometimes they are surprised that two or three wretched little months have not been enough to recover happiness at the jagged end of a two- or three-year affair. How can I explain to them that in-stant gratification is the body's gift? A heart takes it own sweet time to heal. As for women of twenty-four, twenty-five, thirty, thirty-one who are feeling on the shelf and desperate to start a family, true enough, the biological clock may be attached to dynamite, but youth is longer nowadays and families are small. There is time in hand for the making of a baby or two.

Practically all the old clichés about time are misleading. We are not as old as we feel, for example, and sometimes it is too early for some things, and sometimes it really is too late. I feel half my real age, for example, but it's certainly too late to learn Russian, or have the daughter I'd like to have raised as well as my son, or sing The Queen of the Night. I'm just in time for a facelift, but I'll never be a ballerina. 'A Nobody' at only twenty-one is still in slow time, young time, changing time, learning time, healing time. Nothing is finished yet for her. If she will be patient and try, she is in plenty of time to change her mind, to change her direction, to change the way she struts her stuff, and to shake off defeat and depression before they become habitual: she is in plenty of time to change.

Alas, of all the troubled people who come my way, none is more difficult to shake up than the wallower in self-pity and self-loathing. She will bat back every helpful suggestion thrown her way with a cry of 'I can't!' and then retreat to her couch in triumphant lethargy. True enough, some of them need professional help for depression. It seems to me, however, that while an awful lot of treatment uses medication to alleviate the lethargy and self-pity and other symptoms of depression the actual cause is left untreated and unsolved, a brooding darkness marking time between the happy pills.

It is generally held that bad feelings ought not to be tolerated by a good society; books and even whole careers (that of an agony aunt, for example) are dedicated to making sad people feel better. But where did we get the idea we were *supposed* to be happy? Are bad feelings necessarily bad? Feeling bad is feeling too, as I've said before, and the only sure way to stop having bad feelings would have to be to stop feeling at all, just as the only sure way to stop risking bad thoughts would be to stop thinking, and the only sure way to avoid bad experiences must be to do absolutely nothing.

The feeling of grief for example, a bad feeling: isn't it natural and necessary? And can't the bad feeling of anger be useful, creative and crusading? Even 'A Nobody's' bad feelings of neglect and inadequacy have a kind of energy which she can, if she makes herself able, turn around on itself and use constructively.

'My mother was a great beauty,' an eminent woman psychologist told me once, 'and I was so plain, she despised me. Then, when I was in my early twenties, instead of going on moping and feeling sorry for myself and waiting for someone to rescue me, I made up my mind: I had one life, success was up to me, and I decided to go for it. That was when I began to make my way . . .'

We need unhappiness. What else but unhappiness leads us to discover and change *why* we are feeling unhappy? When we feel bad, that's when we have to pursue happiness actively, and in our pursuit of happiness we do our greatest work, we find our greatest challenges, and we discover the cures for what ails us.

Though it has its uses, mood-changing medication, like most easy answers, makes me very suspicious. Every adventurous, hopeful human being needs to feel bad, too, and get to the bottom of it, each time with a little more self-knowledge and a little more good humour than the time before.

'A Nobody' has to find the energy to pursue her happiness. Youth is on her side. But nobody has previously taken much interest in her, I fear. She can benefit from a dose of the agony aunt's ultimate treatment, the most efficacious penicillin in our bag of tricks: the custom-tailored pep-talk. Repetition of the pep-talk is required, I'm afraid, and I hope 'A Nobody' has friends who will pick up my theme and hammer it home. Anyone who hopes to help a troubled friend solve her problems had better work hard on developing her pep-talk. At best, it grabs the attention. At least, it does no harm.

An awful lot of doing good is refusing to do harm.

• • • • • • • • • •

Dear 'A Nobody',

Try this: take pen and paper in hand, sit down and draw up a list right now of every little thing you have ever liked doing, or wanted to do, or can do. Can you — let's say — sew? Can you cook? Can you sing? Do you like long walks? Do friends in trouble come to you? Are you a good listener? Do you like children, animals, old people? Can you write poems? Can you drive, ski, dance, swim? Would you like to learn? Why not? Don't you dare say 'Can't'! If the word 'Can't' so much as crosses your mind, give it the boot. We find ourselves and all our confidence in the things we can do, and want to do. So, to blazes with what you cannot do or do not want to do: that's somebody else's list.

Have you thought about getting up every morning half an hour earlier to do exercises, or read a newspaper, or write a journal? That half-hour can be the first in a new kind of day. You have to start somewhere. And a new day will begin a new week, and a new week a new month, and thus, by starting with one small step of half an hour every morning, on into a new kind of future. It doesn't matter how you begin taking control of your own life, it can be merely by accomplishing a job you've been putting off for ages. Do you want to get around to cleaning out your bedroom closet, for example? Why not now? I mean now. Don't say 'Can't'. A piece here, a piece there builds your confidence and makes a whole picture.

The source of self-esteem is self-confidence. And that's what you need to start working towards. The first steps are always very, very scary. But then it gets easier, and easier, and you'll know you're winning when it starts to be fun.

At twenty-one you are old enough to think about directing those *first steps to lead you away from home. Flight is not always cowardly. Sometimes it saves lives. Why be afraid to retreat from an arena where you are pretty sure you've lost before you've begun? But don't even think about escaping with your dimwit boyfriend or any other who treats you badly — it would be a step in the wrong direction: backwards. Scout around at work and among your friends for possible flatmates, start organising yourself for when you feel you are ready at last to strike out and leave home.*

If I hear you say 'Can't', so help me, I'll throttle you.

It's awful not to like your job. But why not make the job work for you? As long as you are earning from it, let it subsidise your training for something better in the future. Check your list. Choose something and go for it. Just because you've finished formal schooling, it doesn't mean the learning has to stop.

One step, the next step, and when you take a tumble, up you get, and start again. Others see who it is you think yourself to be, so do everything you can to think yourself interesting and busy and terrific: soon, you will know yourself to be all these good things.

By the by, unless you need to lose twenty pounds for health reasons, the only valid argument for doing it is that the change will give you increased control and confidence. You've tried and failed? Well, try again. Don't even whisper 'Can't'; don't even think it. Visit your doctor first, make sure your general health is good, and ask for advice on a sensible diet. Self-confidence has good days and bad days (feeling bad is feeling too and a part of knowing yourself), and I defy anyone to feel on top of the world when in the middle of PMT, flu or migraine. Grab your life: hug it, love it, squeeze every last drop of experience and joy out of it. If you know down deep inside that you need professional help to get yourself started, then ask for it: you're entitled to do that. Tell your doctor not to foist you off with pills. If he or she does not know of an appropriate therapist, try another doctor.

Don't say 'Can't': it's exactly the same as saying 'Won't'. You're not a nobody, you're somebody important. If you won't make yourself a confident life, then who will do it for you? Who can?

Sincerely,
Aunt Irma

• • • • • • • • • •

AGONY AUNT'S WORKSHEET

1. If you could look like anyone in the world, who would it be?
2. If you were as drop-dead gorgeous as she is, would you then stop smoking / biting your nails / eating between meals / putting off until tomorrow / or any other thing you've been wanting to stop?
3. Is it because you don't look like her that you don't stop doing things that make you feel bad?
4. List twelve of your favourite things, things that make you feel good — the month of May, say, or a bubble-bath.
5. When or if you have a daughter, what will you not do that your parents did in raising you?
6. If I were a fairy godmother instead of just an agony aunt and I could grant you three achievements in your life, what would they be?
7. Write a pep-talk.

TEN BASIC RULES
for a (relatively) untroubled life

1. Always keep the real problem at the front of your mind: don't treat symptoms instead of root causes.

2. Do the best you can; never expect anyone else to do better than they can, or will.

3. The only way to change another human being's behaviour is to change the way you react to it.

4. Love is acceptance.

5. Love is never a reason to accept what is intolerable.

6. You are responsible for yourself, but you are not responsible for anyone else over the age of consent.

7. You and you alone are your own judge — be honest, be strong, be merciful.

8. Some problems cannot be solved, they can only be left for time to change or carry away.

9. You damn well can help the way you feel.

10. Nothing can ever again be what it was. Anyhow, it wasn't the way you remember it.